FROM THE HEART
of the
ETERNAL HIGH PRIEST

An Interior Dialogue of the
Redeemer with a Catholic Priest

FATHER EVAN

Queenship

PUBLISHING COMPANY
P.O. Box 220 • Goleta, CA 93116
(800) 647-9882 • (805) 692-0043 • Fax: (805) 967-5133
www.queenship.org

The above symbol which appears with each entry is known as the *Holy Seal* or the IC-XC NIKA Stamp. In each of the four quadrants; there are two Greek letters, "IC", "XC", "NI", and "KA". A cross separates these letters. The letters "IC|XC" are the Greek contractions for *Jesus Christ*. The abbreviated letters for IC (Jesus) are Iota and Sigma. The abbreviated letters for XC (Christ) are Chi and Sigma.

The word "NIKA" is the Greek word for *conquers* or *victory*. The word *Nike* is the name of the Greek god of Victory. The usual literal translation of "IC|XC NIKA" is *Jesus Christ conquers,* or *Jesus Christ is victorious.*

Library of Congress Number # 2005090901

Published by:
Queenship Publishing
P.O. Box 220
Goleta, CA 93116
(800) 647-9882 • (805) 692-0043 • Fax: (805) 967-5133
www.queenship.org

Printed in the United States of America

ISBN: 1-57918-291-7

Contents

Chapter One
Sung Lamentations of His Priestly Heart
Year 2004

Chapter Two
Discourses

Chapter Three
Canticles of Heaven

Foreword

There is no secret today of the problems in the Catholic priesthood. Defections, scandals, lack of morale, lessening of vocations, rebellion and outright demands for a married clergy are frequent in the secular and even the Catholic press. Led by the Holy Spirit, Christ's Vicar on Earth, Our Holy Father, John Paul II, used all the means at his disposal to encourage, heal and develop an ever more committed clergy that is formed spiritually and renewed to meet the demands of an increasingly secularized world. John Paul II's Encyclicals, Apostolic Letters, and homilies, then, highlight the needs of a reform of the clergy. For in every age of the Church, there is always a need for renewal through the power of the Holy Spirit, particularly for Her priest-shepherds.

It is with great joy and appreciation that I recommend this work entitled *From the Heart of the Eternal High Priest*. It is a profound call for a renewal for the ministerial priesthood and in turn for all the baptized, those who share in the common priesthood of Jesus Christ. The author is a Roman Catholic priest writing under the pseudonym of Fr. Evan. I am his spiritual director and every entry was submitted to me under obedience for approval, prior to its' publication. Now this work contains three chapters of dialogues received during the liturgical year of 2004. Chapter One, *Sung Lamentations of His Priestly Heart*, presents 29 interior dialogues with Jesus or Mary that are directed universally to all priests. In Chapter Two, *Discourses*, the Eternal Father, Jesus and Mary direct themselves in a more personal vein to the author in his role as a parish priest. Lastly, Chapter Three, entitled *Canticles of Heaven* is inspired prose for various liturgical feasts.

The major themes of the first chapter are reflected in the opening dialogue entitled, *Come to Calvary*. It begins with an invitation from Jesus to "listen to your teacher." It is an instruction not only of the mind, but also for the priestly heart. Placed before the priest is the sorrowful state of his Espoused, the

Church. She is in "the agony of death." Who is going to revive her? Only those priests who by their complete gift of self to their Bride can help to bring forth this springtime for the Church.

This call of Christ given to all priests, then, is one of conversion, imitation, and union with the Lamb who has given His life for His Bride upon the Cross. For this reason, Jesus asks of each priest an ever greater increase of worship of the Eternal Father through the Gift of the Holy Spirit, a love and devotion to the Holy Eucharist, and a humble openness to our Lady in her role as *Mother of All Priests*.

The passage from the dialogue, *Be Restored in My Love,* is one long cry of Jesus to His priests that they be restored in His love. From that will come a love that is "purified, healed and divinized" to restore His Church.

In these dialogues is a challenge to all priests for a renewed commitment in the service of Christ and His Church, His Mystical Body. On the day of their ordination, all priests prostrated themselves before the altar of sacrifice. This most profound gesture symbolizes the entire gift of the priest-self in loving and humble obedience to the Lord and the People of God whom they are called to serve.

In the beautiful dialogue, *The Sentence of Love*, Jesus urges His priests to remember His call of love in their youth. Their pristine response must be rekindled, made to once more be ablaze in the priest's soul. In that fire is the Lord's presence by the Power of the Holy Spirit. From the priest's heart, like the burning bush of old, the voice of the Lord's "I AM" echoes and illumines all the areas of the Church to be cleansed and revivified.

Fr. Evan's dialogues bring out the love of Jesus for His Bride. As He lives in His priests, so, they too must burn with love for the Bride. That love alone enlightens and illumines the dark, cold world of "no-Christ", of "no-Jesus." For this light of Love "shines in the darkness and the darkness has not overcome it." (John 1:5)

In conclusion, *From the Heart of the Eternal High Priest* is inspired dialogues from Our Lord's desire to possess the hearts of His priests, to receive the surrender of their heart to His own. It is also an invitation to all of His children to a complete surrender of the heart and an ever-deeper renewal. May priests and the laity by their gift of self to the Eternal High Priest, live out ever more fully their respective vocations.

Fr. Francis
Spiritual Director of Fr. Evan
November 2004

Preface

From my first recognition of a priestly vocation, during the many years of my seminary studies, as I lay prostrate before the altar during the Litany of Saints on the day of my ordination, nor even after years as a diocesan parish priest, would I have ever thought that these *dialogues* from Heaven would take place in my priestly life. If asked, I would have responded in the affirmative that Jesus does indeed speak to us in the secret recesses of our hearts and, yes, all of us by our Baptism and strengthened in Confirmation, are given that prophetic call to be a voice for the Lord. But this, this is something most wonderful and unexpected! And so at times, I am overwhelmed by all of it, including personal questions of unworthiness, and even authenticity. I leave this up to my priest spiritual director for his discernment. Of this I know for certain, that my reception of these dialogues has brought about in my priesthood a far greater and intimate identity with Jesus Our Eternal High Priest. As Jesus shared from the intimacies of His Priestly Heart I came to see the power of His Love and Mercy for His priest sons, a power that above all seeks to restore His priesthood.

Hear the longing of Jesus' Heart to bring His restoration, His healing to this most noble of brotherhoods: **It is My most ardent desire to speak to the parched souls of My poor priest sons. How great is My desire to minister to their priestly needs! Only I, the Eternal High Priest of the Eternal Father, can bind and heal the wounds of My priest sons. Day and night I see My priest sons suffer the agonies of doubt, despair, loneliness and isolation, impurity, confusion, every form of weakness, corruption and compromise. I cry out to them, My beloved sons, for whom My Heart is rendered!**

My little priest sons, be restored in My Love so that the Church may be restored from the gift of your purified, healed, and divinized love. Know, My priest sons, I desire your healing and conversion. Will you not grant Me access to your broken and emptied hearts? Will you not let Me revive you with My

Spirit? I speak to you tenderly because My Love for you is tender. Remember the tenderness of My first call to you for priesthood. I am most desirous to restore the tender intimacies of our conversations.

Be restored, My priest sons. Behold, I bestow upon you great graces during these days, graces of conversion and renewal. Be converted from sin; be sanctified in My Spirit. Behold, I who make all things new, I am doing something wonderful in My Priesthood! Come Spirit of Pentecost. I breathe the Holy Spirit upon My priest sons. Receive the Holy Spirit!
I do love you My brothers with an insatiable Love. Your Jesus
(July 26, 2004)

My brother priests, in my love for you, I pray that as you ponder these dialogues that you too may receive such tender heart-intimacies from Jesus, Our Brother Priest. May His Love restore us and may our priestly love then be given in all purity and fecundity for the Bride, the Church.

Fr. Evan
October 2005

Chapter One

Sung Lamentations
of His Priestly Heart

During this last liturgical year of 2004, particularly during the Season of Lent, I received a series of interior dialogues with Jesus by which He most intimately relayed from the depths of His Priestly Heart, meditations upon His Passion and Crucifixion. During these conversations I would receive interior images of the Passion from the viewpoint of Our Savior. It is my understanding that these extraordinary graces were given to me, a weak sinful vessel, from the burden of Our Lord's Heart for His priest sons and the Church during these days of great trial. This dialogue is dedicated, then, in a special way to my brother priests from the Heart of Our Eternal High Priest. May the Eternal Father be glorified in the gift of our priestly hearts in loving service to His Son and the Bride, the Church.

February 4, 2004 – Come to Calvary

Jesus speaks: **My gentle son, turn your ear to Me and listen to your Teacher. I instruct you now as I did My disciples. See to it that you keep company with your Master so that He may instruct you. Now then, know that it is only in the gift of Love** that is the Holy Spirit, the consuming fire of Love that can re-fashion the human heart as a vessel of mediation. Know that alone through My Spirit, the Spirit of My Father, can My Bride be renewed as in fire. Only by an ever-new Pentecost can My priest servants be re-consecrated in the truth and loving obedience. Know that the Spirit's movements are never without fruit. Where the Spirit moves there is Divine Life anew. All is recreated through the Spirit. Over ancient rites the Spirit speaks today in the hearts of holy prophets. Ritual must bring forth a flowering of the Spirit. It is in the hearts of men that this flowering will begin.

Be converted to Me, My priests. Imitate Me in My immolation. Come to Calvary and be affixed to My Cross for the sake of My Love. Here in My school of Love you will learn how to be My priest: My mediation of the Father's Mercy, My mediation of the breath of the Spirit who breathes forth a new Pentecost upon My Church. See, She is in the agony of death. You My priests, resuscitate Her through your seed of complete gift of self. Be wedded to Her alone. Not to the World. Not to the pleasure-pots of this depraved generation. Not to your own self, an idol of self. No, be wedded to Her alone! See, She needs Life! Her womb has become barren for lack of the spiritual generation of Her priests-shepherds.

My priests, I surround you with holy righteous laity who exhort you to holiness and the promises you have made to your Bride. Be renewed in My Holy Spirit. Be priests of My Eucharist. Be consecrated sons of Our Lady waiting upon her every bidding. Be priests who worship their Heavenly Father in Spirit and in Truth. Be priests who bring forth Life! Do not contracept the life that is to come forth from your heart. Feed My Sheep! Shepherd My flock. Protect them from the enemy's camp. What account will you give on the Day of Judgment? If you have not lived for your Bride, then you will not live with Her in Paradise.

Be purified My priest sons. Put on the armor of salvation and deliver My people. Rescue them from the jaws of death. See how the enemy has defiled My Church. Salt the Earth! Clean out the Sanctuary. Re-consecrate My Holy Temple. Give life to the Sacred Mysteries, by your holiness, by your breath of the Holy Spirit. See I will make all things new. The victory is mine. Will you share in My victory crown? Will you be My victors or will you too be defeated along with your fallen brothers? Be strong My priest sons, Knights of the Immaculata, yes? Go forth in My Holy Name and be victorious over the enemy. Be victorious by your abandonment to obedient love. Love your Bride and give Her life.

You are My priests. Bring glory to Our Father. Your Divine Master, Jesus
Amen Lord! Amen!

February 24, 2004 – A Golden Heart

Today I have been experiencing numerous "piercings" as though a fiery blade is thrust through my heart. During the three o'clock hour of mercy my heart felt as if it was on fire and then as if it was being pulled from my chest! Lord Jesus, may I know why You have blessed me with such an intensity of heart piercings this day?
I now receive an image of my heart being encased in gold. Jesus, the Eternal High Priest, places my heart in a golden chalice. My heart, now golden, begins to fracture and crimson blood begins to spurt from various fissures. My own blood begins to fill the chalice. This is my share in the Passion of the One Mediator, to commingle but a drop of my own blood with that of the Precious Blood of the Savior.

Jesus speaks: **My son, see I place your heart in My cup of salvation. Your heart I encase in gold for I am testing your heart, a trial by fire, purifying your heart of all impurities. Only a heart that is golden pure can be broken apart to feed My sheep. As you grow in your perfection of My Priesthood, your heart golden, you are able to fill My chalice with your own** blood, your sacrificial love. **Your love is to be a sweet vintage from My own Vine.**

Lord Jesus please be patient with me, but why am I receiving such strong heart piercings this day?

Evan, this season of Lent will be like none other before, for you. You will receive special graces in your soul. I am tilling the soil. I wish to plant My seeds of faith, hope, and charity very deep within the wounds of your heart. Here they may take deep root and mature. I am drawing your heart to My breast. I long to embrace you in intimacy. I need your surrender, My son! I need your trust in all things. As you release your heart unto Me, I may place your heart fully in My cup of salvation. Let us drink it together, you and I. Let us be inebriated in the sweet elixir of the Father's Love.

My son, remain steadfast and increase your discipline. At all times raise your heart in prayer to Me. I wish to accomplish miracles of grace in you. I will not speak to you tonight of My sorrow over the present age. It is sufficient for you to know that I am raising up the greatest saints of My Reign in your own day. These witnesses will shine forth in glory with such an intensity and clarity. Golden hearts to be pierced for crimson! Do you desire to be pierced, My son?

Yes, Lord, I will it. Pierce my heart for the Kingdom and for the glory of the Father!

I now receive an image of myself in a white-golden dalmatic. I understand these vestments of the deaconate to signify service. I see Christ above me, the Eternal High Priest in a white-golden priestly chasuble. As I look up to Him, I am bathed in a white-golden light and my body is pierced with large white-golden nails. The enemy spies upon this from the edges of the dark shadows and rages, but I am protected in the rays of Christ's light. A nail longer than the others seems to pierce the area closer to my throat. This is where I have experienced very sharp pains, lately. Jesus, what does this piercing signify?

Jesus continues: **Evan, this piercing is for your speech, your preaching. As your heart becomes golden, so will your mouth to proclaim My Truth and Love with sweet beauty. I have placed** over you, your spiritual director. I fill him with wisdom and a stout heart to lead you. Be obedient and submit in all humility. I bless you this night My priest son in a glad embrace. Let us together establish the Reign of the Immaculata. She is your Mother. She gives you a sweet kiss on your forehead this night. Be vigilant My son! Pax. Your Divine Savior Jesus

February 26, 2004 – Stabat Mater

The Blessed Mother speaks: *My children, how sorrowful was my heart at Calvary. My tears exhausted, my love poured out as a libation upon Earth's children. As nestlings I gathered my children to my Immaculate and Sorrowful Heart. As my heart was one with my Son's Most Perfect Passion, here, here in my heart I gather my children. Here in my heart you find your refuge. I am the Refuge of Sinners* (Refugium Peccatorum). *See my love, my maternal guidance refashion your love for my Son, as of my own love; a love that is pure, insatiable, tender, attentive, responsive, faithful, and above all these, a sacrificial love that compels you and I to Calvary's Mount. My dear children can you imagine the horrific pain my heart endured to see my gentle Babe, He who is Innocence, to become as a Sin Offering. With each buffet, with each blasphemy, with each mockery, with each wound, with each curse and defilement My Immaculate Heart was pierced by the noble sword of sorrow, compassion, and co-redemption. As my Son breathed His last breath, giving up the Spirit's breath, my final sword met its mark; my heart cleaved and pierced to become eternally one with that of the Sacred Heart of my Son.*

Know this my children: for every tear, every cry for mercy, every heart bruised, broken for the Passion of my Son, and every heart that surrendered to the Redemption of His Blood along the Via Dolorosa, I gathered all of these precious gems of the merits of my Son's Redemption into my Most Immaculate Heart. On that terrible Good Friday these merits gave me strength and comfort. Now this day as you join with my Son in His Passion, I gather these precious gems of merit into my Sorrowful Heart. As the enemy was defeated at Calvary by the Crucifixion, so the enemy is defeated in you by your own crucifixion. In your death to yourself, you are freed for the Love of my Son in the Life of the Trinity!

My children during this season of tremendous and precious grace let me gather you to Calvary. I do this for you in the Holy Mass in a special manner. Pray too the Rosary. Pray my Son's Stations of the Cross. Meditate upon Our Passion! Here is the wellspring of your love for Our Hearts, Sacred and Immaculate.

My priest son I am your Mediatrix of all Grace! Ask me with confidence for all things. A good mother knows her son's needs. I show you my hands, channels of Heaven's Grace. I wait upon your request, Evan. And with these graces you will be more able to perfectly accomplish my bidding.

Mother, may I always be attentive to your bidding! Our Lady smiles and then I see her mournful as many, many of her priest sons turn away from her! This is the spirit of Jezebel's unholy bidding. Oh, Mother, I am so sorry for your pain, the loss of the love and company of your priest sons. Please Jesus, let me never be parted from Our Mother! My heart could never have it! Mother place the colors of your Mantle about my priestly shoulders. Claim me as your son. Send me on your errands Mother! The errands of Our Father's House!

My son, climb the heights of Calvary, the heights of Carmel, and the heights of Tabor.

I understand this to correspond to suffering, contemplation, and transfiguration.

Mother, lead me by the hand. Let me walk only in your pace and in your shadow. Mother, Mediatrix, open to me the channels of your Grace. Perfect me in the holiness of your Son! Pierce my heart with Heaven's Love. May I be consumed, immolated by the Love of the Hearts of Jesus and Mary. May I stand bravely, lovingly with you at Calvary.

Yes, you will my son. I place my Mantle of sorrow, contemplation, and transfiguration over you. Let us fix our gaze on Mercy's

Wounds. Know that my Son's deepest wounds were hidden: rejection, defilement, hatred, blasphemy, mockery, and indifference. Will you share in my Son's hidden wounds? Will you suffer with a perfection that is hidden and tucked away into the recesses of my Immaculate Heart? Will you stay hidden with me under my Mantle, less the enemy's fury be unleashed against you? For now your time is hidden, yet a time will come that you will be asked to accept my Son's Crown. You will be presented as Love's offering for many souls; one rejected and despised by the world. And in this your perfection will be complete. We will speak of this in time, my priest son.

February 29, 2004 – The Free Embrace of the Passion

Jesus, my Beloved, I am here my sweet Friend. Please continue to reveal to me the depths of Your Heart. Draw me into intimate whispers of Your Suffering, Your Passion of inexhaustible Love. Jesus, I am convinced that at any time you could have ended Your Passion. You were free and in this the enemy brought to You the temptation to turn away from the terrible cost of our redemption. In the Garden it began, then the mock trial, the scourging, the crowning, the blasphemy, the road to Calvary, the lying on the hard wood of the Cross, and the long lonely hours there on Calvary. But You were victorious over temptation for our sakes! We worship You who for our sakes endured temptation and suffering!

Jesus, today as I celebrated the Eucharist, Your rich banquet of Love, my heart was pierced and I was overcome with tears. Lord, may my attentive loving celebration of Your Mass draw others to this Feast of Love, like St. Pio! May I personally attend to You with the ointment of my own most unworthy love for the sake of Your Sacred Wounds and the greatest wound that is hidden in Your most precious Heart.

Jesus speaks: **My son, I greet you with My Hands out-**

stretched to you. I present to you My Most Sacred Wounds. I bear these Wounds that bleed or pain Me no longer, as an eternal testament for the gift of My Love for the Redemption of the Father's children, My brothers and sisters. Yes, you are observant of the movements of the enemy. As I entered the lonely, dark, frigid, forsaken Garden of Gethsemane, so unlike Eden, I entered into the depths of the enemy's camp. My battle ended with that ancient enemy at Calvary, but at Gethsemane I dealt a mortal blow. Here the enemy unleashed all of Hell's fury against Me. He knew the Miracle-Worker could turn away from all that was to beset Him. He tempted Me to find the weight of your sins as all too unbearable. But, you know the depth of My love for you and all of My brethren is inexhaustible. I do not mean to say that this burden did not, however, demand all of My fortitude to endure. I had to give all that I possessed! This was a Victory won only in anguish and burden that came as droplets of Blood. My Calvary had already begun. I was crushed to the Earth by the One who had been cast down to the Earth. That ancient Tempter! I did this so that My disciples might draw strength from Me for their time of trial! You may be brought to a complete prostration under the weight of the battle, with the severity of the temptation. But as I overcame the temptation, so you too will always be given the necessary strength! I stamped upon the head of the Serpent and stood anew; now to leave the Garden not in exile as the First Adam, but in betrayal so that I might take the Fall of Adam upon My shoulders.

March 1, 2004 – The Betrayal and the Arrest

Jesus speaks: **Evan, I bless you for your fidelity to our conversation. Do not be distant from My Heart. My Mercy restores all things. Do you trust in My Mercy?**

Yes, my Master, but I am greatly saddened by the pain I have inflicted upon You by my sin! Jesus, Mercy!

My son, you know well the balm for My suffering! It is your love given, your heart and will surrendered to me. Never let the enemy keep you from applying this balm to My Heart.

I now see Our Lady placing my hand to the Heart of Jesus.

As I stepped forward from the hours of agony in the Garden, I was met by a force that came to arrest Me as one guilty of a most severe offense. And yet, as Innocence, I offered My hands to be freely shackled, to be led away under force and bondage. But I tell you I went away freely. I chose to be handed over to the chief priests and the elders so that I might fulfill the Father's Cup with Love that was freely given. Peter fought My arrest. Good Peter, he felt such a responsibility for his Master. Peter desired above all that no harm would come to Me. He once before had tempted Me to turn away from the Cross and I rebuked the enemy speaking through him. Now Peter took matters into his own hands. He drew his sword in protection of Me, yes, but Peter acted in defense of his own honor, as well. He struck the very organ, the ear, that he had deafened, so as not to hear My message of the Cross. My son, the enemy will strike you and desire you deafened to the call of your Master. The enemy is desirous of you to fight against the scandal of the Cross, as did Peter, the Prince of the Apostles. The enemy will rage against you to fight false accusation, to be led away in shame, mockery, and rejection. Imitate your Master. As your hands are bound and you are buffeted, see the true freedom of your heart filling the Father's chalice with the sweet elixir of your obedient love.

March 4, 2004 – The Hidden Agony

Lord Jesus, send Your Spirit of purification upon me; detach me from material, created things. Purify my heart of all that is not of your will, Father.

    I now receive an interior vision of Judas who steps from the dark shadows of the Garden. He is nervous and fidgeting with his hands. He moves quickly in his betrayal, less he loses his will. As he draws near to Jesus, his eyes meet his Master's. Jesus' eyes are Mercy, yet also great pools of sadness. Judas is cut through to the heart, but still he completes his betrayal with a kiss. Judas then stumbles backwards and quickly escapes into the shadows.

    Jesus speaks: **Let us continue our conversation. Evan, see in My betrayal the sharp sting of the betrayal of friendship, intimacy, and love. I gave Judas to drink from the very depths of My Love; I opened My Heart for him alone to be drawn into intimacy. But Judas came to me with a heart poisoned by greed, by avarice, by pride and rebellion, by a lust for power, possessions, and the flesh. His heart was given to suspicion, doubt, envy, and isolation. He stood out from the other disciples of mine, but My friendship was offered to him in the most genuine and sincere of manner. Do you understand that Judas was not used by Me for My betrayal; he was offered redemption and eternal friendship in full. For three years I beckoned to him and gave him every opportunity to be smitten by My Love. But his heart was in the end given over to the enemy. How this saddened My Heart, to lose one so intimate, one whom I had given everything! Is not Judas the representative of too many of My Father's children? Their hearts are divided as they are drawn to Me. Grace upon grace I pour into their hearts and yet they rebel against My gentle, sweet embrace of Peace and Love and Joy in eternal friendship. The enemy poisons their divided hearts, their disordered passions and desires. The** enemy's cunning in mocking imitation draws their desire for eternal uncreated beauty to transient created beauty. Shiny bobbles, hmm? Lives made for eternal friendship are shackled and strained in the pursuit of possessions. Judas is the human condition of avarice, pride, and rebellion. Yet, Judas is the marker of My Divine Mercy. I call all to My side and to be My disciples. My Love is made vulnerable to the "Judas" in all of the Father's children. All are sinners! All are bestowed inexhaustible Mercy! All are made in freedom, freedom to reject Love's bidding. Free to surrender to the poison of self and the enemy.

As Judas pressed his lips to My cheek, his lips were poisoned from a heart that was poisoned. How his kiss burned with acid upon My skin. This is of the flames of My suffering, My hidden agony to be betrayed; so great a Love poured out and to be rejected. To be turned away for thirty pieces of silver! How many whom I call friends have turned Me away for silver, for earthly, creaturely things.

As Judas came forth from the shadows, so here is where the enemy does his bidding. He hides in waiting, observing, calculating, and plotting; ready to snatch the unwary, those with eyes of avarice, with hearts divided. I send My Angels of Light to illumine this shadow and I call out in Mercy from the Garden to the sinner. But will they see? Will they hear Me? No greater treasure can I grasp in My embrace than your heart, the heart of a disciple that is given to Me in love; a heart pure and singular, a heart aflame with My Love, a heart that radiates with the Beauty of the Life of the Trinity.

My son, be this pure heart. Surrender all to Me and you cannot fathom the grace upon grace that is yours! Shine My Light in the shadows. Dispel the darkness and the fear. See, I cry out from the Garden in My Mercy. Keep company with Me in My Passion. Accompany Me into the depths of My Love. I bless you this day. Pax. Jesus

Jesus, I am an unworthy sinner, but only say the Word and I shall be healed. Speak to me, Jesus, the word that is Mercy!

March 5, 2004 – The Docile, Obedient and Trusting Lamb

Jesus speaks: **I am forsaken! I who had never suffered any physical violence upon My Body, I am now assailed with buffets, strangling with My bonds, shoving, spitting, curses, mockery, and every manner of insult. O how My senses were assailed! I uttered prayers upon My lips for My attackers, My brothers whom I love and I cried out to My Father! Father, am I abandoned? Am I forsaken, am I removed from Your Loving presence? From the Garden to My last breath at Calvary the Father removed His saving presence from Me. He who was always present to My human soul, was now removed! In My hours of such desolation and cruelty, I was so terribly alone. It was the Father's will so that I might embrace all of human suffering in My Redemption. Further still, My Passion was to be the gift of My Love to the Father.**

It is a gift that I invite My disciples to partake in. You are to be My sweet comfort, My healing balm in the midst of My Passion. My eyes cry to you in Mercy. Extend the mercy of your heart to My Passion. Let yourself sink into the depths of My Sacrificial Love. Together we comfort one another. We speak together of Our Father who is Goodness, whose Mercy endures to the thousandth generation.

In My obedient Love you find the strength that you will need to be handed over and stripped of everything, so that you might be a fragrant offering of love.

Lord Jesus your greatest suffering during Your Passion, as You have shared, happened in the hidden recesses of Your Sacred Heart. But why would the Father's presence be removed from You when You needed Him the most? What does this mean for your disciple?

My son, I allowed you this day to but glimpse obscurely into My Sacred Heart at the depth of My suffering. In this

My Passion, I give to My disciples the perfect example of Love that is purified and strengthened. A beautiful Love, yes? It is a love that knows the Father's loving presence and mercy in the very depths of the heart. A love that then is returned to its source and in this holy exchange, it is in turn extended to the mirrors of My Love, the children of the Father. Yes, I was hidden from those who inflicted harm upon Me. My Divinity was veiled, just as your birthright was hidden from those who have caused you harm. And what was My response? As they beat Me and tore My flesh to pieces, My lips and My Heart did not cease to speak of Love. Rather, My suffering only fueled to enflame My Love for them. For when true Love realizes it comes at a great price that Love is as a fountain that will not cease, no matter what the cost! Through suffering your love is strengthened for your Enemies, for all your brothers and sisters. My Passion and your suffering, your compassion purify your sacrificial, agape love.

And yes, in the midst of My greatest suffering the Father's Love was sensibly removed. In that dark night of the soul, the Victim Lamb looks upon the altar pyre and cries out for deliverance; not My will, but Your will, Your cup I choose to drink! Will the torch strike the wood? Will the hammer be driven into the nail? Will the Father reveal His face to Me in this hour of suffering? To be a victim lamb, one knows what they are, a victim lamb given to a loving worship in sacrificial love! The lamb is docile to whatever the Father wills for glory and redemption! The lamb trusts in all that the Father does, for in the depths of his being, he knows himself as loved by the Father.

The lambs know that they are never truly abandoned; forever they are to be embraced by the Father's Merciful Hand. Will the lambs stay in this embrace? Will they trust even when all is dark? When all seems as loss? Only if the lambs will recognize and heed My voice. My son, rest this day in the peace of a lamb curled up at the Father's feet. Let the enemy not tempt you to distraction. Trust in Me! Trust in the Father!

Thank you Jesus, My Paschal Lamb.

March 7, 2004 – Hidden Glory

Last night I suffered a most severe attack from the enemy. For hours I fought against the enemy. I called upon Jesus, Mary, Pio, and then finally through my Guardian Angel I was able to find some peace and sleep. I understand, that in part, this was to develop my relationship with my Guardian.

I am left terribly weakened by the fray. My head feels as if it has been struck many times. I now receive an image of myself collapsed upon a pillar to which my hands are bound. I am being struck about the head and upper back with rods. I do not protest or struggle. I endeavor to endure it with a loving trust. Jesus, may I possess Your countenance to endure all suffering with grace and not to count the cost.

Jesus speaks: **Evan, we move now into My physical suffering. I have allowed you to experience but a small taste of the rage of the enemy upon My flesh, My spirit.**

Lord Jesus how little I could endure last night before calling upon my Angel to rescue me! I cannot fathom how you endured such unspeakable suffering from the enemy!

My son, I drank fully of the Father's chalice to the last drop. His love sustained Me to the Victory. My Mother too imparted her strength into my weakened limbs. In their faces, the blows, the spitting, the curses, the hatred and rage of the soldiers and temple guards, I encountered Satan acting through his agents of torture and cruelty. With each blow, with every disgrace against My hidden glory, I uttered prayers for my offenders and won many souls to the Father's Kingdom. I endured more so that I might win more to My side!

My son, do you desire to win more? Paul, My Apostle, encourages you to "run the race to win"! (1 Cor 10:24) Receive My fervor for souls. In your suffering at the enemy's hands and lips, in wicked hearts and malice, in injustice and disgrace, you

can win many souls. Let not a drop of this precious grace be wasted! Be poured out and know that I never leave your side. I cheer you on even if you cannot sense My company. Run to win! Win not for yourself, but for the glory of the Father and the love of souls! Yes, My son?

Jesus, how limited has been my sight. So infrequently do I offer my suffering, the enemy's attacks, for the winning of souls! Rather, I move all too quickly to crying out for mercy: Rescue me O Lord!

Jesus, I beg of Your Spirit the courage and fortitude to run so as to win!

My son, trust in Me. I will know when to strengthen you and grant rest and peace. And I will know when you are to take up arms again and when to be bound and scourged for love of Me and of souls. I bless you this night. Rest well. Jesus

Jesus, You honor me with your loving conversation. May I honor You by bearing much fruit from Your Words!

March 10, 2004 – The Rejection

I receive an image of Jesus and I standing over a pit to Hell, a temporary opening. I see many, many twisted human forms clamoring towards this opening. I cannot describe the overwhelming sense of dread, violence, and chaos that arises from this abyss. Jesus rolls a stone over the gap and seals it with His Sacred Heart. It is His Heart alone that seals the gap between Heaven and Hell. It is the choice each soul makes before His Sacred Heart, to surrender to the force of His Love and the Divine Will or in rebellion to reject a holy submission to such Love.

I now receive an image of a vast crowd of humanity, as if every square foot of the earth is covered with a sea of humanity. I can see into their faces, their desperation, their cry for mercy and redemption. Their limbs, faces, and clothes are soiled from sin and its effects. Jesus allows me to see their need, my need reflected in their faces. And what will be my response? Will I turn away from this need? Will I try to minister on my own? Or, will I wisely lead them to the Good Shepherd? I receive a final image of myself leading a vast throng in the desert to an oasis. There is a tall date tree and the people begin to eat ravishingly of its fruit, the fruit of the oasis in the midst of this desert exile. I understand the Eucharist to be this fruit, this Bread, in the midst of this earthly sojourn.

Jesus speaks: **Evan, we continue. I am bound and brought before Caiaphas and the hastily assembled Sanhedrin. They stand together as a single line of opposition. The enemy sneers with disdain and mockery through their faces. How My Soul, My Will is crestfallen. In Love and Mercy I had called My brothers back. I alone offered them resurrection from their whitewashed tombs. I poured out My Heart in prayer, in Mercy. And now I am dragged as a common criminal before them. I cannot bear to look upon them for the weight of My sadness.**

I am now moved by the Spirit to weep from the very depths of my soul. O my Jesus how You suffered so!

But I look into their eyes and My eyes of Mercy search their souls. Some, a few, can I reach and they will reject the mockery of this trial. They face scorn and rejection by their brothers. How brave these souls; great is their reward! To defend Christ!

But, alas, the enemy has closed the ranks. As one body they press upon Me with lies, distortions. Poisonous venom spews from their hearts to their lips. The enemy has blackened their souls with greed and compromise. They cannot, they will not endure the Son of Man. I cannot speak of this crushing blow. Such terrible rejection from the religious leaders of the People chosen apart and espoused in Covenant and the Torah, the Law! As My Heart is rendered, I speak of My Divinity, of the promise of My Resurrection and coming again in glory! I reveal the Father's plan in all of its fullness. My Heart is rendered, yet are their hearts moved? Can they surrender to such Love? Can they reject the enemy's death grip upon their soul? No! They

render not their hearts to Me, but render their priestly vestments in protest. They will not serve the Eternal High Priest! Their priesthood has fallen in service to the lord of darkness. There is no more to be done. I have extended Mercy and Truth and they have chosen the father of all lies and eternal desolation! I have done all that the Father has asked of Me. I have opened My Heart and My Kingdom.

This sadness, this grave rejection!

I opened My Heart, first, for the Chosen and the priests of Levi. At the Last Supper, in My Blood, I established My Eternal Priesthood. Until the end of time I beckon to servant-shepherds to follow Me in priestly service. To each, I again bare My Heart. I open My Heart to My priests, so that they might be drawn to Me and from My Heart alone shepherd My People. I make My Heart vulnerable to My priest-shepherds. I call them to an intimacy of infinite proportion, so that they might act in My Person and in My Authority and in My Love.

But so many of My priest-shepherds heed not the cry of My Heart. They close themselves off to the Son of Man and the submission of their love to My own. How My Passion continues through My priests. How I am saddened! My son, you for a time closed your heart to Me. I became a stranger to you; I who had called you to this exalted vocation. I will bless you in your surrender to My Love, in your defense of the Christ!

My son, gaze upon your priest brothers with My eyes of Mercy. Speak to them of the Love of their Eternal High Priest. Will you not ease My sadness? Will you not help to return to Me the hearts of My priest sons? Your Jesus

Yes Lord, but teach me how! I struggle greatly with priestly bonds of fraternity. Make of me a new creation. Jesus, I thirst to co-redeem with you, to suffer with you, to bring relief to Your suffering.

March 1 4, 2004 - Prisoner of Love

My sweet Jesus, I beg you, please do not remove your affection-
ate embrace from me! How cold is my heart! How weakened is
my soul, sick with longing. Jesus, I desire to be fully immersed
into the flames of Your Love! Consume all of me, Lord Jesus, by
Your Love that purifies and enflames the empty cold recesses of
my heart.

Blessed Mother, comfort me! Hide me within your home at
Ephesus. Gently, patiently instruct me of your Crucified, Resur-
rected and Ascended Son. May my heart be wounded by His Love.
See that nothing remains of Evan! Let only Jesus' Heart live in me,
Mother. Restrain my wicked tongue, purge my fleshy desires, raise
my eyes to beauty that is lasting, and compel my heart in charity.
Strengthen my limbs, Mother!

Jesus speaks: **My son, surrender all to your Master. Do not
hesitate; do not be distracted from coming to My Eucharistic
side that is pierced for your sake. See My saving waters and
costly blood pour forth for you to drink abundantly. My son,
here is where you belong, in My Company. Give yourself over
to me. Let our embrace echo in your heart. Let your heart cry
out, Here is my Beloved! He comes to me! He dwells in me!
His abode is my heart!**

My Eucharistic Lord, as I pray before Your Blessed Sacrament
my heart is gravely saddened. Is Your Heart saddened, Jesus?
There is such an intensity of sadness present to me! Why Jesus
are you sharing this with me? How may I bring You the balm of
my love? I now receive an image of Jesus in a small dark prison
cell. He is bound. It is the night of his arrest and He is alone, so
terribly alone.

**Yes, My Son, I am saddened. I am alone in this prison
cell. I am held captive by My Love. I am bound by Love to
this small cell. I await My trial before Pontius Pilate. I cannot**

sleep. I am thirsty. My face is bruised, My eye is beginning to close shut from the pounding of their fists. The smell of the cell is of human waste. I am alone. My Father's presence as you now know, has been withdrawn from Me. What awaits Me I know is in the Father's will. The rope is cutting into My wrists, the circulation to My hands is being shut off. My hands are numb. I am so weary. I am in darkness and I await the dawn. My prayer is constant upon My lips. Father, strengthen Me. Father, bind Me in Your Love. Father, I surrender all that I am to You. Father, I will pour out My Blood as a love offering for their sakes. Please Father, rescue Me from this Hour. Let Me not be deprived of Your presence. I have become a sin offering. Receive Me! Receive them, Father!

Here in this prison cell, I surrendered Myself as Love's captive awaiting execution. The Cross I bore was to be alone, held imprisoned. I knew My poor disciples suffered greatly. They ran like stray dogs, hiding in shadows, whispering in the dark for familiar faces. Strike the shepherd and the sheep will scatter! How I desired to comfort them, to give them words of encouragement and peace for their troubled souls. Poor Judas! Poor Peter! I prayed fervently for My sons, My brothers that they would not be lost, but drawn to My Cross, drawn to the glory of My Resurrection.

In this holy tabernacle, I too am a prisoner of Love. By Love's ties I am here in this prison of love. I whom the Heavens cannot contain, I who could have shattered the walls of My prison cell that night with but a gentle breath, I came to be contained, to be secured here behind a locked (tabernacle) door so that I might be made accessible. And here it is that I await upon the dawn; the dawn of souls hungry for My Presence, bowed in humble adoration of their Victorious Lamb! But yes, My Heart is saddened too, here in this place (tabernacle). How few visit the Divine Prisoner of Love. How few keep Me company as I am bound in Love. How many commit sins of indifference, of sacrilege against My Blessed Sacrament.

Like My Apostles, so many of My children scatter from Me. They hide in shadows. They speak in fearful whispers.

The enemy pursues them and they are confused, exhausted, and frightened. But they do not come to Me! They are easily lost and distracted. They forget that I am here, their Prisoner of Love to calm their fear, to speak My Love and My Truth, to raise up their fallen spirit.

My son, become My prisoner of Love with Me! Bring to Me My dawn by your loving presence and I will open to you My Heart. My son, as you pass my prison cell do you not feel the wound of Love in your heart? I cry out and often you pass Me by. Keep company with Me even if for a short time. Comfort Me in My sadness. Do not waste your hours within the prison cell of the enemy (television and computer) that entraps and does not free. Only My prison cell of Love frees! Thank you for spending this time with Me. I bless you My child for you have strengthened Me in My sadness! Love, Jesus

Jesus, how blessed I am to spend this time with You in Your Most Blessed Sacrament.

March 15, 2004 – My Enemies Surround Me

I am suddenly quite overtaken by dizziness and exhaustion. I am forced to retire at this hour of mercy. As I am offering my suffering in prayer, I hear Jesus speak: **Evan, I desire to take you deeper into the mystery of My suffering. Please write for me.**

But now I am overcome with doubt! I am fantasizing! I am delusional! I am weak and sinful, Jesus would never reveal to one such as me, the depths of His Passion! My heart, however, is being strongly pierced even as I write of these doubts. Jesus, thank you for this confirmation. Jesus, I trust in Your Goodness and Your Love. May I not be deceived. I desire to trust in You! I am open to receive. Yet, I can barely write from my vertigo. Guardian Angel, please assist me!

My son, in your suffering, in your loving embrace of all that is to come to you, I wish to write My Gospel of Love, My Passion Song. I take you with me, My son, to Calvary, to share My Cross, for herein is your perfection! Herein is My Love for you!

Jesus, would You please speak to me more then of Your Passion?

Dawn comes this good, terrible day. The day of My atonement, the day of My Self-offering. The Victory of the Lamb, the enemy's defeat! I awaken stiff and exhausted from a brief rest. The temple guard is at the cell door. As the key enters the lock I pledge My Love as the key to unlock the Doors of Paradise. I pledge to the Father to give all that I am this Day. I draw from the final seconds of solitude with the Father, before I am drawn into the hurried, cruel rush of the tempest of My Passion. The guard, My own kin, treat Me roughly as they pull upon My fetters, like a dog they lead Me. I am brought before Caiaphas and the chief priests, the scribes. They do not address Me personally, but speak of Me as a curse, a defilement, a blight to be wiped away from their inheritance. I am pushed and shoved as we begin our procession to the Roman Authority.

I who came to save My own, I am being turned over by My own! If only they would see My hidden Divinity they would cease this cruel betrayal! But all is as it is, for the Redemption of all. All have a part to play. As I walk upon the earth and feel the soil, the dust beneath My feet, I am pierced to the Heart! I will redeem all of creation. The enemy's kingdom is at an end! I am now attacked by fallen legions. With each step, I find My limbs heavier and heavier. The chains pull upon My ankles and I feel as if I am dragging the weight of the entire world. I bow My Head in fervent prayer to My Father's Angels: strengthen Me! Guard over Me, less I dash My foot upon a stone.

As the gates of the Roman Court are opened I am met by such an onslaught of cries! Such hatred, such rage is unleashed upon Me. I am stunned! Again I am pushed and pulled into the courtyard. The crowds press upon Me as one body. I am spat upon. Stones are thrown at Me. I search the crowd for My

Mother. Her arms and her heart are outstretched to reach Me. The guards keep a barricade about Me. Her heart is pierced for Me. I lose My breath as I look upon her grieved face. Mother, who bore Me and held Me in her arms, My Co-redeemer! Let us strengthen one another. My supporters are few in the crowd. Monies have purchased My enemies and My accusers. The betrayer, the ancient enemy has swollen his ranks with many in the crowd this morning, but My Blood is to be shed for all! The noise is deafening, the press of the crowd surges upon Me. I feel so weakened! How can I stand to bear it? I who walked freely among them and taught openly in the Temple, I who gave them bread and fish to eat. I worked miracles and cures in their midst. How they have turned against Me! The enemy oppresses Me without mercy through them. I am brought to the steps of the Procurator. Here we pause as the case against Me is presented.

Father I pray, bring Me to My Cross. How I long to embrace My hard Altar, to spill My Blood for their redemption. Their words wound Me by their blasphemy and deception. I desire only to surrender to their torment. O that it would begin! Strengthen Me, O God. Calm My trembling hands, let them embrace openly the nails of salvation!

My son, in your weakness, in your exhaustion keep your hands open to accept with complete surrender the perfecting embrace of My cross. Keep company with Me. Your Jesus

Jesus, place me as Simon of Cyrene to assist You with all my strength and courage!

March 18, 2004 – New Wineskins

Today I feel utterly exhausted. I prayed my Office from bed, but now I am before the Sacrament of Love. The enemy continually disturbs my sleep such that I am each day forced to throw myself at the feet of Jesus, His Mercy and strength to compel me, to revive me! Jesus, through Mary, receive this day my every good action, thought and desire. I consecrate my suffering so that it might become redemptive in Your embrace, Jesus. Grant me victory against the enemy. St. Joseph, Terror of Demons, pray for me!

I hear Jesus once again: **Evan, let us continue this, the memories of My Passion through My human Priestly Heart! How this age in My Church needs the Words of My Priestly Heart! Above all, for the ministers of My Eternal Covenant, I desire to form you in this seedbed anew, to have hearts consecrated in service and love to your Eternal Shepherd. My Mother's mediation for her priest sons never ceases before the Courts of Heaven. She is your Mother-Intercessor, your Mediatrix! My priest sons pour out your troubled minds, hearts, and your very souls to her! She gathers her priest sons and fondles you upon her lap. In this maternal intimacy she banishes the darkness, the desolation, the sadness of My priest sons. Her embrace, strong and intimate, banishes the enemy!**

I am brought in procession once again from the Roman Court to the puppet-king, Herod.

I now see narrow passageways. Jesus keeps His Sacred Head bowed. He is gimped by the short iron fetters about His ankles. He is shoved roughly before Herod. He does not meet Herod's gaze.

I keep My gaze downward. My prayers are not to cease! I must be strengthened. My feet are bound, My step is narrowed and the guards push Me roughly to hasten this exodus, to lead Me away from their midst, the midst of the Promised Land. And yet I alone in prophetic fulfillment may lead Israel to the Land flowing with milk and honey.

I am brought before Herod, the blood of John still fresh upon his hands. His court is an empty coffer, no riches for the Father's Kingdom! It procures only vice and death for the land of Israel. I, the King of Kings, stand before a mockery of kingship, of lawful authority from on High. I do not meet the gaze of such mockery. My work now is in My own Blood. This is My Kingly blessing. It is a sad end to the line of Kings

of the Chosen People, a people, a land ravaged by the enemy. Chastised, purified, but never forsaken! I AM in their midst, to be raised up as the Eternal Kingly Priest.

I am mute to Herod's mockery, to his kingly demands. My only conversation is interior. I speak to the prophets and righteous kings of old, of the inheritance of My Father prepared for them. I am the last Prophet to be taken before a King of Israel. No longer shall they hear the prophet's voice. Forever will the prophet's voice be vanquished from this court! But My Truth will live forever! It is a sad end to the final chapter of Israel before the Age of the New and Eternal Covenant. But behold, I gather the fruit of My Vine into new wineskins.

My priest sons, will you be these new wineskins? Will you bring My Harvest to a ripened sweetness, an exquisite vintage pleasing to the Owner of the Vineyard? Gather My Harvest into your hearts! These are My new wineskins; priestly hearts in union with the One Eternal High Priest. Empty yourselves of all that is of your self and of the snares of the ancient enemy. Humbly pour out yourself, disposing of your old wineskins, your hearts withered, cracked, and bitter. Give yourself over to My embrace. I alone can create of you a new priestly heart, one of My own making; one large enough, tender and pliable enough to hold My Harvest.

My priest sons know that what you produce is not your possession. It is not your Harvest. It is not of you, it is only through you, in My goodness and favor. Be humble first, my sons, and you will begin to know My Priestly Heart; I who emptied Myself completely to become the Wine of the New and Eternal Covenant.

My sons of My Priesthood, pay no heed to the "Herods" of your day who mock and defile your priesthood, your kingly role. Keep your heads bowed in humility and fervent prayer to the Eternal King who reconciles all things to the Father. Trust and listen to My Priestly Heart. **Your Rabboni, Jesus**

Lord Addonai, create in me a clean heart O God, an upright steadfast spirit. Do not deprive me of Your presence, but embrace me, so that I may possess the love and fortitude and wisdom to be poured out as a living libation! Your priest-servant, Evan

March 23, 2004 - Holy Obedience

Lord Jesus, I know that You want me to always move forward, to not be set in old ways and habits, but to be open to whatever path the Spirit will lead me. May I be free of all impediments for a complete docility to the Spirit. May I desire to die to myself, especially in all the comforts and pleasures that I am accustomed to.

Jesus speaks: **My little priest son, I have kept you waiting upon your Good Shepherd. I alone know when it is to profit you from this revelation of My Priestly Heart. I alone will move forward the timing of this conversation. Do not doubt, do not fail to trust, but do not stop your ardent prayer for My Voice, either! This holy desire on your part will increase the charismatic gift of Faith. Long for the gifts of the Lord, for the sake of the Body!**

Now, I am once again pushed and shoved in procession to the Roman Court, I knew that My Hour approached. As a young boy I taught in the Temple for three days. I instructed the elders through the Spirit from on High. I the Ancient of Days, a mere boy, amazed these leaders of learning and piety. As I spoke of My Father's Kingdom, I too was being instructed by the same Spirit. My Body, not yet the body of a man, was to become both the Temple of Worship and the Temple of Sacrifice. In this young Body I alone was to reconcile all things to the Father. In My young limbs, I was to bear the wounds of all sin. In My Body I was to bear the weight of all humanity. In obedience I surrendered My Body from this young age. I returned to Nazareth to submit to the authority of Joseph, our Holy Guardian, and Miriam, My sweet Mother! In this I obeyed the Father. In My obedience to authority My limbs were

strengthened. The tools of My trade honed My muscles, but My will was hammered into purest gold by holy obedience.

As I pass the Temple, My will quickens, My limbs spring forth. Forward! May I accomplish Your will Father. Your Spirit fortifies Me. Let My Hour be upon Me! The Spirit has strengthened Me through obedience. Do you understand this My priest sons? Your limbs, your will, will be strengthened by holy obedience to the Will of the Father as revealed through the Spirit, in My Word, in the Authority of the Church, in your religious superiors, in the law of charity, in the duties of your priestly office.

From the first moments of your awakening until your exhausted slumber, in each moment and hour, holy obedience is elicited from your priestly heart. Will this day be marked by obedience and the sweet company of the joy of abandonment or will it be one of constant resistance: self over God, flesh over spirit, pride over humility, pleasure and comfort over service? Mark well your morning offering my priests sons with a conscious surrender, that this day may the Father be glorified by your loving surrender to His Will. May you be as a finely ground and sifted wheat. Let not your disordered desires, attachments, and your seduced will, push away My Cross. But in gentle trust hasten to embrace the Cross anew each day. In your conscious holy submission, your limbs will be strengthened. Your will shall become purified in a golden docility. Your own priestly bodies will become temples of adoration and temples of sacrifice. Hasten now your steps, my priest sons. My Hour has come. Your hour approaches. Let us run to embrace the Father's Will. Be glorified Father, be glorified.

Surrender all impediments, the littlest of disorder. For here, even here, the enemy will clamor to maintain a viscous foothold. Unleash him to the foot of My Cross; let him not be bound in any way to your will. Be free, Evan! Be free!

Have courage; see in your sufferings the intensity of My Love as I draw nearer to you. Do you welcome My Sacred Heart, My Sacred Wounds? They are one in the same; both are the Door to Eternal Life.

Thank you Divine Master. Rebellious will of mine, be conquered! Submit to Divine Love. There is nothing sweeter, no more perfect gain! Submit!

March 25, 2004 – An Immaculate Love, Joyful and Sorrowful

I receive from an Angelic Messenger: *Gather Earth's children this day. See present this saving event in your salvation. The Messenger of Heaven's Court, Gabriel, gives holy tidings to the fairest of your race. She is the Holy Immaculate One, all generations to call her blessed. She is holy obedient solicitude. She waits upon her Master's bidding. Her entire being is open, open to receive His Word. In her receptivity to the Word of God, she is overshadowed by the Spirit's very Being and the Word becomes enfleshed in her own flesh. She is "bone of my bones and flesh of my flesh". (Gen 2:23)*

Her being now is the Holy Tabernacle of the Most High God. She like the Israelites of old, brings forth the holy dwelling place; her holiness like the flame that illumined the night. The Holy Spirit overshadows her as the cloud overshadowing the holy tent. She is the dwelling place of God! Come let us adore the hidden presence of the Most High in her womb, as we adore the hidden presence of the Lord in the Holy Eucharist. Holy Mary, reveal to us the Word made Flesh.

And Mary said: "Behold, I am the handmaid of the Lord. May it be done to me according to thy word." (Lk 1:38)

Blessed Mother, we rejoice in Heaven's tidings this day. We share in Gabriel's joy to bear greetings of Heaven's message for you, the Chosen Daughter of Israel, who one day will be the Queen of Angels! Gabriel's Queen!

As I am praying my Office, the Queen of Heaven is desirous to share a word. She waits upon me as I invite her to be my prayer partner and together we finish the Office. Mary speaks on this glorious Feast of the Annunciation: *My gentle priest son, please write for me. I bless you this day, this beautiful Feast of Heaven and Earth, this glorious Feast of Joy! Heaven's joy to behold the Eternal Son now Incarnate. The obedient Angels had for endless ages longed for this moment, to sing in glorious adoration of the Word Incarnate. Their voices, each a distinct hymn of adoration, that echoes through all of creation, all eternity. Let him who has ears listen to their beautiful anthem of praise. Gloria in Excelsis Deo! Glory to the hidden Divinity enfleshed in the womb of a Virgin!*

Let us also speak of my assent to the Father's most loving perfect plan of salvation. I did not fear, I did not doubt in God's Hand that day. His Hand alone fashioned me for this honor, His Hand alone could bring to fruition such joyful tidings. In this holy and wonderful tiding, I gave my trust, my yes to the Spirit who had always been with me. As the Spirit spoke in me a humble obedient faith, my yes, my fiat allowed the Spirit to overshadow my entire being. Here through the breath of the Spirit and the Hand of the Creator Father, the Eternal Son was implanted as a Seed of Eternal Life. The Word made Flesh!

Such exquisite joy for me! For every day that I carried in my womb the Holy Infant was a continual Holy Communion. He who was to become our Eucharist, our reception of hidden Divinity, now dwelled in me! The Ancient of Days now took up His abode in my lowly body! Imagine my joy, the grace of my continence to be a living tabernacle. In this daily communion my love of Jesus grew in such intimacy. I spoke to the Holy Infant within my womb in constant holy conversation. In His Love made vulnerable, I became His Mother. My yes to Jesus, my love of Jesus, and I speak of ineffable mystery here, would carry me to the Cross. Jesus was to carry me as His Cross to Calvary, for I am immaculately conceived by the merits of this same Cross. But it was a Cross that I too was to be transfixed to by Love, by the ineffable mystery of suffering born of agape! Love that gives of oneself to death! His wounds became my own at Calvary. As our bodies were one at the Annunciation in bonds of flesh and love, so now my body, my Immaculate Vessel, was one with the Incarnate Flesh of Jesus at Calvary. My heart, my love are split open so that my body, my love immaculate might be one with Him.

Know this my priest son, as you surrender to the same breath of the Spirit to be overshadowed in Mercy and Love, that is Jesus, know that you will bear Him in your flesh borne of suffering! Here your will, your body, your love will become one with His. There is no other way for my Son to be reproduced in you, for Eternal Life to be borne in you!

As they took my Son away in heavy irons, so my Immaculate Heart became as if imprisoned by the weight of this separation. 'To bind their kings in chains, their nobles in fetters of iron; to carry out the sentence pre-ordained this honor is for all His faithful" (Psalm 149:8-9). *I stood in that empty Temple, my hands outstretched in prayer. My womb now empty like the Temple; empty of the One Teacher, the One King, the One Eternal High Priest, and my body shuddered for the absence of His presence. As Jesus was absent of the Father's presence, so I too entered into the desolation of His absence, of the cost of redemption that awaited the Holy Flesh I bore. My flesh. My blood. Such sorrow for the Mother of the Redeemer, your Mother! But the gentle Spirit moved me from my desolation to strength, the strength to be affixed as one in my Son's suffering, in His death.*

The joy of our love on this Feast of the Annunciation and the sorrow of our love at His Passion are one in the same, borne of the same heart united to His Sacred Heart. Learn from me. Learn of the union of Hearts, Sacred and Immaculate. Bring glory to your Father's House this day. I love you. Your Mother, Miriam

Mother Miriam, may I attend to you this day, my Queen. Give to me the honor of waiting upon your bidding, you the Handmaid of the Lord. *Salve, Maria! Gratia Plena! Dominus tecum!*

March 26, 2004 – I Remembered Love

Jesus, please speak to me of Your Love in the intimate breath of Your Passion.

Jesus speaks: **Evan, let us continue our conversation. Yesterday you bestowed honor upon our Amma[1] on her beautiful Feast. How eager she is to share from the depths of her Sorrowful Heart particularly for her priest sons, who too often wander afar in darkness and are the constant target of the enemy. My son, please pray for and reach out to your brother priests.**

Jesus continues the Passion.

They have taken Me to the Praetorium. I am filled with a new measure of strength from the Spirit. My Sacred Heart is overflowing with ardent charity. Would that I could fly to the Cross this instant, but all is to be fulfilled according to Scripture. I their King, their Noble Companion, I am brought before the crowds in iron fetters. As I look upon My children, My sheep, My Spirit and My Body shudder! How the enemy has turned their hearts against Me! He mocks My Atonement. For these You die, for what gain? They have already rejected You, they have refused Your Love! Why suffer torment for the likes of these?

And then I meet My Mother's eyes. Her eyes are darkened by her nightlong vigil of prayer and tears. She is My strength this Hour. For this reason was I born of her flesh, for this reason I came into the World, to become Flesh given up for the Life of the World. The enemy is powerless to dissuade Me. My Mother's Mantle hems Me in. She is My Sweet Mother.

The crowds begin their jeering at the prompting of the High Priest. They cry out for My Blood, for My death by crucifixion; a death for criminals, for sinners. There is no appeasing their thirst for My Blood. See how the Father allows and uses the

---

[1] *Aramaic* for mother.

enemy's movements! For all of God's children shall thirst for My Blood and all shall desire My death for the salvation of the World. The enemy's movements, his deceptions have reached a fever pitch. Their sound is deafening. It is the onslaught of the enemy's voices, the incessant buzzing, assailing one's peace. Only in My bonds, My bonds of obedience do I find My peace. I surrender to their embrace, knowing that by them I will be led to the place of scourging, the flaying of My Flesh for the sins of the world. I leave this crowd, thirsty for My Blood as lions to a kill; the jaws of death envelop Me, but I am not forsaken!

My son, will you lend me your courage, will you share your back, your limbs to the whip of the enemy's scourge? Will you, like My Mother enter into My Passion? Will you assist Me in Love?

Lord Addonai, I do not shy from the sting of the whip or the executioner's insults. But I wrestle alone with that untamable, rebellious will of mine. Even in the sight of the spilling of Your Blood, the flaying of Your Flesh, the enemy stokes up the coals of rebellion! Let me not be like the Israelites of old who fought against You, but grant me the grace of Joshua, to enter the Promised Land with Your armies of Light!

Jesus continues the Passion.

A tether is pulled from the iron fetters upon My wrists to an iron ring upon the pillar. I am pulled up so that My feet barely touch upon the earth. Already I am being raised up as the Cup of Eternal Salvation.

Lord Jesus, what prayers came forth from Your Priestly Heart as You were about to be scourged?

I remembered Love, the unspeakable intimacy of the Love of the Father and the Son. In My Heart I lifted up Joseph, My Guardian Father, whom I longed to be with. My Mother's Heart was present to Me, it overlapped My own. Her love never left Me. I looked upon My Apostles, My Priests of the Eternal Covenant. They received My special portion of Love. I had taught them after My own Heart, the Heart of the Redeemer: hungry for souls, risking all to save the lost, compassionate towards the weakness of man, fearless in the face of the enemy, and above all to be sons obedient in love to the Will of the Eternal Father. My Mother's Heart has been moved by My Love of My Priests. She shares in My intimate Love for these elected vessels. My son, will you pattern your heart after Our own? Will you love your brother priests?

Jesus continues the Passion.

Before the first blow upon My Flesh, I unite Myself to the Father; Body, Soul, Mind, and Heart, all of My Being.

I see a great golden light appear from the Heavens upon Jesus affixed to the pillar. I believe it to be from ministering Angels.

Nothing can steal Me away from this embrace. Is this not true for you My priest sons united to the loving Will of the Father? What harm can come to you? Though they would seek to destroy your bodies, your reputation, your good name, your place in this world, if you endure all configured to the Father, never can harm come to your soul. You are held as a babe in the bosom of the Father. And I alone am the Way, I alone can bring you to the Father. Do you not believe Me, that this is the pulse of My Heart's beat, to bring My priest sons to the Heart of the Father?

I see Jesus press his forehead upon the pillar and tears stream down His cheeks.

You My priest brothers are at the center of My Heart! The choicest portion has been allotted to you. Will you surrender your love to the Heart of your Redeemer, who in His Love for you surrendered His Body to be flayed for you? Will you add your weight to the executioner's whip or will you be the sweet balm, an ointment of Love? Come My priest sons to the Heart of the Eternal High Priest. His Heart is aflame for you! His Body surrenders to stripes for you!

My son, share My Priestly Heart with your brothers. Their need is urgent, yes? I bless you this day of My Passion. Be reconciled and be one with the Father's Will. Your Master, Jesus

Jesus, my Beloved, I am humbled to know of Your love for Your priests! Would that all of Your priests never forget the dignity of their sacred election for it is the very honor of Your own Priesthood, Jesus. Forgive me now for the countless times I have sinned against this dignity. Your sorrowful priest son, Evan

March 28, 2004 - To Suffer the Stripes

I am resting in bed after Sunday Masses and I am urged to get up and write for the Lord. Jesus speaks: **Evan, My son, write urgently for the call is urgent! I beckon to My priest sons to come to me as John the Beloved, to approach Me in intimacy and to lay their head upon My bosom. Close your eyes. Let your hearing focus only about My breathing, the pulse of My Heart. Know the pulse of My Heart. My priest sons this is what I call you to emulate. Be humble, be docile; listen to your Master. Let your priestly hearts become as My own and live your priesthood from this Priestly Heart of Mine.**

I am overwhelmed by extreme vertigo, nausea, and weariness. Jesus, should I continue writing? I desire not to error.

My priest son, you are experiencing My own weakness the morning of My Passion. I have been standing in heavy shackles for many hours. I have not slept, nor drank, nor eaten. The enemy has robbed Me now of all My strength with his constant assaults. I let My Body sag against the pillar for strength. It is cool to the touch, as I am stripped of My robes. Father, I suffer all for their sins, their redemption. Accept Me now as their atonement. I bare My Flesh for their transgressions, by My stripes are they healed.

The enemy's legions infest the Roman executioners. They are worked up into a sadistic fury. They drool with anticipation to strip My skin, My flesh from My bones! The first strike comes with such force and strength from the rod held high in the air, it is as if all demons have lent their weight to this blow! My wind escapes Me from the pain. I feel the reverberation

to My bones. The force and their rage shock me, but I do not scream out. I abandon Myself to the Father's embrace. I know that there will be many more blows. I fight against fainting from the pain. I must feel each blow to My Flesh. My suffering must be complete. My breaths come heavy and quick. I am straining to regain my breath as each ferocious blow shocks My breathing.

I receive an image of imps with razor-like teeth biting into Jesus' flesh, beginning at His shoulders. There is a pair, one on each shoulder, biting repeatedly and spitting out His Flesh!

I receive blows from each side of Me. Each is competing with the other to inflict more cruel damage from their swing. They wear themselves out upon My back and they are replaced by another pair who begin to strike My legs and feet. I think upon the embrace of My Mother for Me, as a young child. Within her arms I was safe from the enemy's assaults. She was My refuge when I was afraid. I feel her arms embrace Me now. She whispers in My ear of her love and her strength. She blesses Me with her presence.

My priest sons, in your priesthood have you dared to expose your backs, your legs to the cruel treatment of the enemies of the Church, My Body, both within and without the Church? Have you dared to suffer the stripes of mediation, penance, absolution, and charity for those who sin against you, who inflict upon you grave injustice and harm? Will you bare yourselves, your back, and your heart for the sake of souls? Or do you refuse the pillar of suffering, chastisement, and obedient embrace? Are you a noble race who rejects the weakness of your King, in your arrogance and your station? Is your palate scornful of such disdain, of such cruel means? I tell you My priests, surrender your pride for the sake of souls and to save your own! Do you not know the weighty burden, the cost of your priesthood? To whom much is given, much is expected in return. What profit is returned for your arrogance; your lavish lives of comfort; your empty speech that edifies neither God nor man; your perversions; and your abuses of the gift of your body to the Church? I tell you to repent of your old ways while there is still time. The time is urgent!

Do you not feel the groaning of the Church in the pains of labor? She is ready to give birth to a new era in the Spirit, a springtime watered in the blood of martyrs and the righteousness of My saints. My sons return your hearts to Me before it is too late! I will give you the grace; will you give Me your obedience? Give Me this I beg you and all will be created anew in your priesthood. You cannot know what new life awaits you. You will simply marvel in the miracles of grace I will work in your priesthood. Be that new wineskin. Cast off the old! It is wretched and will not be used in My new Harvest.

Jesus continues the Passion.

I again must fight to stay conscious. Every inch of My skin is being bruised, then torn, then ripped with their sharpened hooks. The enemy can see My bones and he is desirous to crush them. Anything to keep Me from the Cross! My Heart embraces My torturers. I forgive them, these pawns of the enemy. There is a respite and the soldiers roughly turn Me to face outward away from the pillar. I am then shoved roughly against the pillar and the pain shoots up My spine. I keep My eyes open now and look up to Heaven. I have turned the other cheek and I surrender to war waged upon My chest. Here is where I welcomed the sinner to draw close to Mercy. My Sacred Heart is exposed to injury! This is the cost of Mercy! Mercy comes forth in Blood!

I can see My torturers now: the cruelty, the malice, the ugliness in their faces and in their limbs. It is the face of all sin. All sin has cost Me pain in My Sacred Heart exposed, in My limbs made vulnerable. I look upon these My sons, My brothers. My Heart speaks to them through My eyes. I AM forgiveness. I AM Mercy. Put down your arm of resistance.

My priest son, in the face of your enemy be My instrument of charity. Harbor no anger, no hardness of heart. Take your enemies into your priestly heart. I have given you a new heart, one large enough, pliable enough for friend and foe. This is the victory over sin. Surrender them to Me.

In my scourging the enemy had his first taste of the spilling of My Blood, but it was not enough. He desired My death, My destruction. Follow Me in your priesthood. Be My holy martyr for souls. Do not recoil from the pain or injury, but always forward to Calvary! Be faithful in all things. Your King of Martyrs, Jesus

Lord, I bless You for Your holy Angels who give me the strength to continue in this revelation. I love You, Evan

March 30, 2004 – The Two Crowns

Jesus speaks: **Evan. Evan. Evan.**

Yes Lord, Your servant is listening. I now receive an image of Jesus from His Cross fixing my limbs to a cross. He beckons and many gather.

Jesus says: **They are thirsty. Give them to drink.**

I can do no other thing than unite my heart to the Father. May I be poured out so that others might live! Jesus, teach me to be poured out each day in my priesthood.

I now receive an image of Jesus suspended from the scourging pillar. His flesh is torn and bloodied. I see Him a good distance away, as if through another's eyes, for Jesus appears unconscious. The chain is loosened from the pillar ring and Jesus is let down roughly upon the base of the pillar. He is prostrate, face up, with His waist lying over the square base of the column.

Jesus speaks: **As the last scourge is brought to My Flesh, my Head, I lose consciousness. I am aware of ministering Angels gently guiding My slumping Body to the ground; rest, a respite from the agony of the pain. But almost immediately My Body is dragged upon the pavement, opening wounds deeper, tearing at loose pieces of flesh. They drag Me by the iron fetters that cut deep into My bruised flesh. My pain jars Me into consciousness. My agony continues. I am dragged into the heart of the** enemy's camp and I am propped up for their mockery. There is no rest for the Son of Man, no place to lay His wounded Head. As I drift into prayerful abandonment offering each wound to the Father, the soldiers are urged by my tormentor to inflict yet greater injury.

Again they raise their rods to strike at the Shepherd. In mockery of the rock struck at Meriba and Massah by Moses, the priest-lawgiver, they strike the Rock many times over, about My Head. Repeatedly they strike My Head and yell their insults, spitting their fury, their rage, and their hatred at the Son of Man. Even as My Head is tossed about I see My Father's children behind the ugly masks of the enemy. They are small puppets pulled this way and that by greater demons. My Love is sent forth to them, My enemies. But their thirst for vengeance will not be satiated; let us not just strike His Head, let us pierce His Head! Let us drive our screws into His skull. Let us inflict our wickedness upon Him. Let us enter Him! Then, I see it, the crown, the vicious crown of the enemy. I see for a moment, an angelic procession of the Crown of the Father to be given to Me. It appears in place of the enemy's crown. In My docility, in My humility to suffer this mockery, I will inherit the Crown of Eternity for all of My subjects. There is no greater honor the Father gives to Me! To reconcile His children, what cost would not be paid? Their redemption at any cost! And so I surrender to this mock coronation.

So now Satan will inflict his crown upon the Head of the Incarnate Word. He wills to pierce his marks upon My Flesh, to mar My beauty, to scar as ugly that which is beauty to be adored. His claws of wicked defilement sink deep into My Flesh, into My skull! This crown was not placed with somber regality and precision by the Loving Hand of the Father, it was hard pressed in mockery, sloppily, in haste and with such force! Everywhere My Head is pierced and each wound is on fire with sharp pains that strike deep into My nerves. As these mock attendants to My Court stand back to 'worship' one marred and smitten, their anger only swells up the greater. "He had no form or comeliness that we should look at him, and no beauty that we should desire him." (Isaiah 53:2)

Is there no doing away with this one? Imagine the ancient enemy's hatred for the Son of Man—for all eternity, exiled in disobedience. It is a malice that is a cancer until there is only darkness and malice. There is no light remaining to My Lucifer. My Lucifer is gone. Now there is only the eternal prince of darkness and his hatred rages against Me. They mock Me with an emperor's robe and beat Me mercilessly about the Head. My Sacred Head surrounded on every side, they drive their thorns deeper and deeper. My sight is lost from the blood that pours into My eyes. My thirst increases for souls.

My priest sons who I gather to My side, listen to Me and observe the treatment of Your King. I suffered unimaginable ignominy, pain, ridicule, mockery, defilement, blasphemy, every terrible thing at the hands of the enemy whose hatred for Me knew no limits! Every insult, every wound inflicted came with the sting of malice, treachery, and wickedness. Satan hates your King. This you know, but do not forget My elected vessels, his hatred for you is of the same measure, the same degree. For in your soul you bear the eternal seal of the Most High Eternal Priest. Satan spies into your souls and sees Me! Know that he seeks too your destruction, your end! He unleashes his legions against you so that you too might not make your way to the summit. How many of My priest sons have been lost to his treachery, his deception, his wickedness. These priest sons of mine suffer eternal defilement as chained dogs who suffer every humiliation by such a cruel master!

My sons be vigilant! I cannot bear to lose another son to the enemy! The enemy is always spying, calculating, and measuring his snares for your capture. Only in the company of My Priestly Heart, only walking in the Spirit of the Father can you see what snares lay about you. My sons you suffer treachery, ugliness, rejection, malice, mockery, every evil thing and you wonder wrongly: "Why such things would happen to me?" I tell you this again, if they hate Me, they will hate you. The enemy and all of his legions, his servants hate you. You are targeted for destruction, to rip your flesh apart, to grind your bones into fine powder. Woe to you priests who do not recognize the snare laid for you. Woe to you priests who have crossed into the enemy's camp. You "Judas's" will come to the same end!

My faithful sons do not fear! In the Company of your King, crowned with thorns, you will receive an eternal crown of victory from the Hands of your Priestly King. Will you wear My Robe of Passion? Will you suffer your pride to Me and know My glory through humble docility? My priests I love you. You are My own, My own image in your eternal soul. Victory to My priest sons! Your Jesus

All hail Our Victor King! We bow in service of Your perfect humility and obedience!

April 1, 2004 – The Lavabo

Jesus speaks: **Evan, My Hour of sentence has come. How I thirst physically, yet My thirst for all souls is unquenchable. I struggle to stand on My own. My hands are bound and My feet are now bruised and swollen. My soles are shredded. Each step is agony. My body shivers from waves of pain, every inch of My skin is marred. I do not give up. I begin to straighten up and the enemy sensing my resolve kicks Me from behind so that I fall roughly upon the pavement stone. My hands are not free to take the blow. My shoulder, face, and head are struck as I fall. The soldiers gather around Me, their long figures hiding the light of the sun, their shadows are darkness. Repeatedly they kick Me and strike Me with rods. One places his foot upon My crown of thorns and steps sharply. The enemy desires to crush My Head, but it is not yet My Hour. One of the guards, you know him, is moved to pity and assists me to stand. They are content for now to process Me to My sentencing.**

The agony of each step! My legs feel as if cast in stone, I

have no strength in My limbs. The roughly hewn cloak rubs against My wounds. As I am brought forward some are moved to horror and shock. Many mock My appearance as the fury of the enemy infests the multitudes gathered. The crowds press upon Me, the condemned criminal. Their thirst for blood sport is excited as they look upon My appearance. My son, I AM hidden, am I not? I could call down a Host of Heavenly Angels to rescue Me, but this is the Son of Man, one rejected, a sacrificial offering for many.

I am brought before Pilate. Our eyes meet. I am Mercy for the Procurator. I am Mercy for his sentence, his office. He is stunned and angered at My appearance. He was not prepared for one so marred by hatred and malice. He presents Me, The Man, to the Court of Israel, and to My own inheritance. The Man. I am all of humanity. I have taken up into My Person all of the children of Man, Adam. All are configured in Me, but not all will chose to be of Me. In My humanity I am hidden so that I might carry out the sentence pre-ordained, that I might bring life to the exiled children of the Garden. I will restore all. I will reconcile all. I will redeem all. But though all are offered salvation, many refuse it. They refuse it in the face of One so hidden, so marred in appearance. They reject salvation: its need, its origin, and its source. The spirit of anti-Christ has possessed their hearts, minds and souls. At the prompting again of the High Priest, they cry out for My Blood to the last drop! "Crucify Him! Crucify Him! Crucify Him! Let us be rid of this troublesome One who vexes us, who disturbs our consciences. Away with Him! Leave us! Let Him be forgotten!"

But none shall forget Me! I AM the Lord of Hosts. I Am the Alpha and the Omega. The Father's glory shall be bestowed upon Me. Now, a criminal is released in their midst, an enemy of the common good, of the people, in exchange for the Ancient of Days. Goodness sacrificed for evil.

Pilate ritually washes his hands of any stain of guilt, of culpability. I Am the Victim Lamb, the offering of Atonement who takes upon Himself all guilt, all culpability, and all sin. I will be washed clean by My own Blood. My priest sons, in your

lavabo you pray: "Lord wash away my iniquity and cleanse me of all my sin." **My sons do you ascend to My altar of sacrifice with a clean heart, clean hands? Have you been purified of sin to act in the Person of the Eternal High Priest who offers the Sacrament of Eternal Salvation? My sons, My priestly vessels, let not just your hands be washed as the Levites of old, but let your hearts, your minds, your very souls be cleansed in the Sacrament of Mercy. Unburden your sinfulness in the confession of your sins. Be humble My priest sons, be washed in My Mercy. Let your holiness shine before the Assembly. Approach My altar in grace, a clean conscience, and as an overflowing temple of the Holy Spirit. Your people, your flock thirsts for holy priests, priests formed in My own Priestly Heart.**

My son, as I took on all of the weight, the burden of the world, so too remember to offer the Holy Mass: mediating, bearing the intentions, the burdens, and the sins of the Assembly. Remember your priesthood. Act in My Person. Mediate the Father's Mercy and Goodness.

I now receive an image of *Ecce Homo.*

My sons, never be ashamed or timid of your priesthood. What an unfathomable honor has been bestowed upon you, completely as a gift, never merited, for it is My own priesthood. It comes from the Hand of the Heavenly Father alone! Does the scandal of your brothers vex you so that you would hide your priesthood? Do the insults, the jeering at one so marred, and a condemned criminal in our midst; does this weaken your love of Me, My priests? Is your spirit, your resolve, your fraternity weakened?

I stand before you, *Ecce Homo*. Will you not stand as one, in solidarity with me, as a sacrificial offering to be poured out? Do you not know My Priesthood, My sons? What deception, what trickery has taken you away from the company of the Son of Man?

Courage My sons! Run to win the race! Reject your comforts and your seclusion; be a priest vulnerable for the sake of the Gospel. May you count it as every honor to have them say of you: Behold the priest! In Mercy, I am your Jesus.

Surrender pride. Surrender safety. Surrender esteem. Surrender to the Christ, scourged and crowned with thorns. Thank you, Jesus. Evan

April 2, 2004 – The Sentence of Love

On Fridays during this Lent I am experiencing intense pains to my head, most unlike a normal headache. It feels as if holes are being drilled into my forehead and temples. The pain seems to last about three hours and I am reduced to tears from its intensity. Every syllable I utter is as if a hammer is striking my head. I am barely able to open my eyes and to write. Jesus, give me the strength to endure! For love of You Jesus and for love of souls; beautiful, beautiful, beautiful souls, do I willingly suffer.

Jesus speaks: **Evan, please write for Me. My son, I stand facing the crowd as One condemned to death. I will become Death: death to sin, death to eternal exile, and death to the eternal enemy. There are no snares for the Son of Man. There is only the loving willing acceptance of the Father's plan, the path, the place of the Redeemer this Good Day. I found great strength and consolation in this Sentence. As Pilate turns Me over to the guard for crucifixion, I see plainly the path before Me. How blessed to know the Father's Will and to carry it out with obedient love, yes?**

I look to My Mother in the crowd. She is comforted by the beloved disciple and My daughter, Mary of Magdala. My Mother's eyes reveal the depth of her own passion. Mother who nursed Me! Mother who fondled Me upon her lap! We go this together, You and I. I carry the beam and you carry Me in your heart. I give My limbs to be nailed to the Tree and you give your heart to be pierced by the sword. I surrender My life's breath and you surrender your Son into the embrace

of the Father. Mother, let us prepare ourselves, let us move in haste for the Angel of Death comes to take the first born Son this night. Let us celebrate this Pasch, the Blood of the Lamb to be splashed upon the Door of Sheol. For those who are dead are now brought to Eternal Life. Come forth the righteous children of the exile; see the Promised Land prepared for you, a land flowing with milk and honey. Come children of My Father to your eternal inheritance! See, I unfasten your chains of eternal slavery. Cross now the river of death. Ascend to the holy mountain, to the holy dwelling place of the Most High God. Rejoice this Day, for your Savior, who becomes Death, will bring forth Life! Rejoice! Mother, let us finish it. You will be My strength and I will be your Champion. My Mother nods to Me her consent; her fiat brings her now to the Way of the Cross.

Jesus, there are so many sharp pains to my head. Please strengthen me to continue! The pain is so excruciating. Jesus, how did You find the will, the strength to continue, for the crown of thorns was only a small portion of your wounds! How Your Love compelled You! What wondrous Love is this! This, Your greatest act of Love! Configure me precisely in this Love, Lord Jesus. No other measure, no other sort of love will suffice for your priest-servant!

My beloved, this is My Love that conquers Death itself. My Love conquered My bodily death long before My last breath upon the Cross. My Love compelled Me. I would not succumb to death before the appointed Hour. My Love compelled Me! My priest sons, to what will your love compel you? Will your love compel you to Calvary in your priesthood? Will it compel you to daily embrace your Cross? Will your love compel you to have a shepherd's heart for the flock, My little ones? Will it compel you to not count the cost, to move beyond the pain and suffering, so that others might have eternal life? My priest sons, to what, to whom does your love compel you? My sons, taste of My Love; it is not bitter. It does not leave you empty or saddened; it does not empty you of your dignity, or disturb the harmony and peace of discipleship. Do you love Me, my sons? Do you love me above all else, more than your self, more than the little things you cling to? Let nothing keep you from My Love. Let nothing keep Me from your love, My sons of My Priestly Heart! How I thirst for your love. For whom did you become a priest? Remember; remember the call in your youth, the call from My own Love for you. Rekindle this Love, My sons. Nay, be consumed by this Love! Be ablaze with ardent love for your Master! Let your love for Me compel you, My sons! This love will compel you to see My Presence, whom you love, in all you minister to in your priesthood.

My sons, My Mother and I move now to the Via Dolorosa. Will your love of Me compel you to follow with us? Come My sons, My Love beckons. Live in My Priesthood. Live in My Love! Come! Jesus, your Love

Jesus, truly Your Priesthood is of perfect Love. Teach me Jesus in this school of Your Love. May my priesthood be an office above all one of love.

April 5, 2004 - Monday of Holy Week & Chrism Mass -
The First Steps

Lord Jesus, in union with Your Priestly Heart I pray that I may be given sufficient grace and possess the proper disposition in body, mind, soul and heart to once again renew my priestly vows this night at the Chrism Mass. May this renewal bring a fresh outpouring of the Holy Spirit. May the Sacramental oils flow anew: oils of sanctifying grace that I may be a pure priestly vessel, oils of charismatic gifts that I may be poured out in building up Your Church.

I ask now My Lady to be with me, to pray on my behalf, so that if her Son might have a Word to share with me, her littlest son, I would be open to receive it. I bless you Mother for honoring my request!

Jesus speaks: **Evan, who can deny any good request of Our Mother? My priest son let us now begin our ascent to Calvary. During this Passiontide draw close to My Priestly Heart. Do not suffer a single distraction, yes?**

Yes, Jesus. I will my attention to be singular this week.

I am led before the crowd and I am now with the company of two public sinners. I am one in solidarity with the sinner. I suffer no shame, no humiliation on behalf of them. I count it as pure joy to reconcile the sinner. To be this Reconciler, we must be in the company of sinners, yes? These two condemned men are fastened with irons to their beams. There is to be no escaping their sentence. The soldiers look upon Me in such a miserable condition; I am barely able to stand, let alone to walk, to escape into the crowds. I am not chained. I am in the Father's providence given to freely embrace My Cross. It is balanced for Me and it awaits My embrace.

I receive an image of many demons darting about the Cross.

My son, the enemy directs his minions to assault Me, to terrify Me of this hard wood, of its coarse embrace to My wounded Body, of its humiliation to the crowds. But I am not tempted away. Rather, I see it being held for Me by My Father's own Angels. It is an honor to have placed upon My shoulder so noble a duty, so sacred a beam. Love of the Father compels Me to embrace this sweet bed of rest, My instrument of final surrender. With Love's force I place My Body under its weight and lift it. Such a burden!

I see the soldiers mock Jesus and laugh at the burden placed upon Him. They cry out: "There is no way He can carry such a load!"

It is placed upon Me as a mockery by the soldiers. "Who are these little people of Judea that would think they could have any other King but Caesar?" **The enemy through their mockery, their disdain of the Chosen One, sought to crush Me in My first faltering steps. But these men do not know of the strength of so noble a Love. As an invisible tether of My Heart pulls Me to Calvary, I take My first steps. The soldiers are outraged!** "Who is this Man? Who is this One so noble that we cannot break

Him! What a will He must possess! Let us increase our cruelty upon Him!"

They roughly shove Me from behind and to My right. My balance is lost and I fall cruelly for the first time. I fall flatly upon My face. My nose is crushed as the weight of the beam falls upon Me. The crowds begin to mock Me as a mighty one who has fallen. "This is no mighty savior of ours! How can He save us if He cannot save Himself?" I am crestfallen under this weight, this burden. My vision is blurred from My injury. Within the depth of My Being I hear My Father's voice: "Onward, My Son, arise!" I feel Life breathed into My Body and to the amazement of My punishers, My tormentors, I arise with the burden of the beam upon Me. I begin again My tentative steps to Calvary. I feel for each stone with My ravaged feet. Try as I may, I am unable with My hands to relieve some of the sharp burden of the beam from My shoulder. Its weight buries into My flesh. Upon My first fall, deeper wounds are inflicted from the crown of thorns and once again I cannot see from the Blood that covers My sight. I move onward of My own.

The soldiers are anxious to quicken the pace, to ruin Me upon the stone path. "Let us finish Him here!" They whip Me over and over again. They bark into My face as horrific beasts and spit upon Me. I keep My Heart in constant embrace with the Father. I am oblivious to their insults, their cruelties. I will not be distracted from My end, My loving surrender to the Father's embrace at Calvary's Mount. I know My Mother is near. I feel her heart quicken and racing to embrace Me with each step.

The enemy trips Me up and once again I stumble and fall. Mercifully I fall to the right and the weight of the Cross goes down first. I fall and rest upon this bed of death. I am whipped repeatedly and the crowds press in upon Me. "Is this not the end of him?" A wave of disdain comes over the crowd as I begin to stir. I arise and again I am given roughly this beam to embrace.

Evan, My priest son, write for My priests. See now as I picked up My Cross in the company of sinners, I led them along the path to eternal salvation. I uttered no cry of protest, no complaint. I did not turn away from this noble task. My priest sons, search your hearts. Have you become one with sinners by taking the burden of their souls upon you in the Holy Mass - the eternal merits of Calvary, in the holy counsel of confession and the directing of souls, in compassion for those weighed down by the heavy burdens of their sin and suffering? Or have you become immune to their cries, their needs? Have you allowed your hearts to become hardened and cold? What deceptions has the enemy convinced you of; that you are to be a pampered minister of grace, a part time cleric who can find an easy escape route from the pressing crowds. My sons, learn from the holy priests who have gone before you. They were poured out as a living libation. They counted it as honor and joy to serve My Body as My priests, My mediators of My Mercy.

Courage sons, the road is long and narrow with many turns and snares set before you. Go, onward! I accompany you. Trust in Me, I have gone this way before you!

My son, we will continue this My path to Calvary. Bring My blessing, My love, My presence to your brother priests. Reveal to them My Priestly Heart. Your Jesus

I bless You and thank You My Savior, My Conqueror of my death.

April 6, 2004 – Tuesday of Holy Week - **The Immaculate Sentry**

I see a woman dart from the crowd at an opportune moment as the procession of the condemned comes to a slow stop. There is a bend in the Way to the left with a steep increase. She comes from Jesus' left side bearing a square cloth folded about two feet square. It is off white in color. Ever so gently the cloth is touched to the

Master's face. She cannot see where the wounds lie beneath the blood for it is so heavily caked on His face, particularly about His forehead and eyes. He has also bled heavily from His nostrils. She can begin to see His eyes. Her heart is pierced by the Mercy that meets her gaze. Her hands tremble with the sacred cloth that she has now brought to her bosom. She slips back into the crowd before the guards take notice. Jesus, such a beautiful kindness Veronica has shown to You. May my love always be as tender for You!

Jesus speaks: **My sight is clearer now and I can see the faces of the crowd. I see the compassionate faces along with those who spit curses and defilement. For those who love Me and for those who reject My Love I move onward.**

I see a woman ahead that looks like Mary, but she becomes a giant serpent wrapped around a tree. She hisses and strikes out at Jesus.

I see one like My Mother in appearance but it is not her. It is anti-Mary, it is the spirit of Jezebel. She is perched upon her tree. Her haughty form flaunts her desecration of womanhood and the seduction of man. She too shall be conquered on Calvary's Mount. It is as if all the gates of Hell have been emptied out onto this path. They are disguised in hooded cloaks and keep pace with Me. They spy upon the One born of a Virgin. Their defeat is near. But behold they cannot pass this point for here stands the Immaculate sentry. She waits upon her Son. She is Woman. She is the New Eve who now vanquishes that ancient serpent. Her Heart Immaculate, consecrated in love to her Son, stands guard. The enemy dissipates into the shadows. She who is humility in perfection crushes the head of the serpent with the strength of Angelic armies.

I see Our Lady in black robes. She is off to the right above the crowd. How profound her sorrow!

Mother of Mine! My Heart leaps at the sight of your holy presence. Mother you are My every sweet comfort. Your grace transcends the ignominy of this cruelty. My Heart is so free of this burden for the moment; it is you and I in one another's secluded company in Nazareth. How blessed were our days alone together, such indescribable sumptuous feasting upon the

Father's Love in our midst; the Holy Spirit crying out within our souls like the shrill cry of a swallow. Truly Our Hearts were immersed in the beauty and joy of Our Company. But now Mother, Our Hearts will become one. Do you not feel your Heart leaving your very body to become joined with Mine? There at Calvary through the iron nail and the Blood and Water poured out as Mercy by the lance's thrust, Our Hearts are eternally joined. The New Adam, the New Eve, Their Hearts are now eternally One in the embrace of the Father's Loving Plan.

Mother, how blessed, how perfect your surrender of your Son to the Father! Your trust speaks the perfection of your love. Your arms outstretched both give the Son to the Father and reach out to share in this burden as Co-Redemptrix. Mother of Mine! How beautiful is the sacred Crown that awaits you. I by My Resurrected Body will place this Crown upon the Assumed body of the Queen of Heaven and Earth!

Mother, see Our infant Church struggling for breath in the midst of this delivery by Blood and Water. Give Her breath Mother; teach Her to breathe in the Life breath of the Spirit. As a mother hen, gather My Disciples who have scattered in their fear from the sharp talons of the enemy. Protect them and strengthen them for their path to Calvary that lies ahead. I will entrust one to you in a special way, Mother. This is My gift to you!

I see Our Lady's face radiate with the Light of the Holy Spirit. Her Heart Immaculate burns with such intensity that rays of light emanate from her bosom. She is Grace and Beauty now more than ever through the depth of her co-redemption. The enemy spies upon all of this from a distance and moves within the Roman guard to roughly shove Jesus as He pauses before His Mother. Jesus stumbles to fall again upon the hard stone. Such sorrow for our Mother!

My priest son, see her who will be *Clothed in the Sun* is now clothed in compassion and sorrow. She bares her pierced Immaculate Heart to Me in her love and she does this for her little priest sons! She looks upon you and sees in your sacramental consecration her Son who ascended to Calvary with the burden of all mankind upon His shoulders. She is moved to loving support and encouragement for these her little priest sons. As she gathered the scattered Apostles into the folds of her Mantle, so she now calls out to you. She looks for you in all of your hiding places. How her Heart aches to show you the depths of her love. Her Heart is pierced by the sword for each of her priest sons! But see, she is little and her presence is so hidden, so beautiful is her humility. Have you lost sight of her Mantle in the crowd? Call to her, Miriam! My sons, surrender to the embrace of this Mother of Ours! She alone will guide your steps most perfectly and surely upon this path to Calvary. She alone will strengthen your limbs for crucified love. She alone will prepare your heart most perfectly to become one with the Resurrected Priestly Heart of your Master.

My sons, she is so small and hidden, do you not see her, her beauty? Become little, my priest sons, in your docility and humility. Then your Queen will be seen. She will come to you, supported on the wings of Angels. Immaculate Mother, reach out your arms to surrender these priest sons to My embrace and to encourage, strengthen them on their path to Calvary. Remain in My company this day. Your Master

Jesus, how beautiful is Your Mother, the Mother of my priesthood! As you entrusted Your beloved disciple John, his name meaning *God's gracious gift* to Your Mother, You gave unto her a true son by the adoption of her Immaculate Heart; such consolation for Your Mother who now surrenders the only Son of her womb to the Heavenly Father's embrace. She receives John indeed as the gracious gift of her Eternal Son. Young John, clothed in the priestly garments of the Eternal High Priest, now is received into the Heart of the Mother of the Redeemer. And until the end of time, Mother Mary's Immaculate Heart is solicitude, compassion, and love for all of her priest sons, who bear the image of Her Eternal Son. Mother Mary, your embrace is sweetness. Your embrace brings forth the tears of a son who knows he is truly loved. Mother Mary, you are mine and I am totally yours! May I serve you always as God's gracious gift! Evan

April 7, 2004 – Wednesday of Holy Week - **The Holy Women of Faith**

Hail my Savior! Blessed Mother, through your Heavenly intercession send now to me your Spouse, the Holy Spirit, to fill every atom of my flesh, every longing of my heart, ever thought of my mind, and every desire of my soul. Jesus, may I simply be completely present to You.

Jesus speaks: **Evan, My sweet little son, see I recreate you with the heart of a child. A child who trusts in their loving parent, a child open to the wonders of creation, a child who converses with Angels as rapidly as men. Remain this child; it is the gateway to great grace. Now, let us go along the Way, yes?**

Repeatedly I am to be pushed and tripped cruelly under the weight of the Cross. Repeatedly I am to fall. Yes, the burden is great, but the enemy's cruelty is greater! I tell you, his malice and hatred far exceeds the sins of Earth's children. For here (the sins of man) **there is weakness and imperfection, while the enemy's rebellion is perfect malice, perfect hatred. Satan is unleashed in all of his fury upon Me. It is in the Father's most perfect permissive Will. The ancient enemy is lured to his doom at Calvary's Mount. Here My Love poured out as Blood, will conquer his hatred and malice. No longer shall its sting rule the Earth and her inhabitants. See how the master of deception is blinded by his own fury, as to his own demise. How terrible is the fate of the damned, to serve one so vile, such a perfection of darkness and cruelty. His cruelty is to be eternally fueled by his malice and hatred.**

My priest sons, have you forgotten this real danger to those of your own flock? Of whom did I speak against and his kingdom? Of whom did I warn and speak of his tactics? Who

did I defeat at Calvary so that victory would be given to My lambs? My sons do not fall prey yourselves to the deception of the evil one. He is like a prowling lion looking for all that he might devour and he begins with you, My priests! My sons, be spiritually sighted, see the enemy and his work plainly. He tempts many successfully to think he does not exist or is not powerful or a danger. Did I not teach all of this as false, as contrary to the Truth?

My priest sons, as I carried the burden of the Cross, My Church upon My back, so you too have been given this sacred duty; to protect as your own, to carry safely the Sheepfold, My lambs. You as the shepherd must keep a sharp eye for this hungry predator. Know his cunning ways. Keep guard and be vigilant for he never sleeps! You do not keep guard alone; do not fear. See, I appoint My holy Guardians about you and Our Lady trains your arm for battle! My priest sons, the enemy has stepped up his final assault. Many of My lambs are falling prey. Will you allow this to happen? Will you not speak plainly of the enemy in your midst, in the sheepfold itself? My sons have courage; be zealous for the salvation of souls. Protect My flock. Put on the armor of salvation!

We continue on the Way. See now the good women of Jerusalem. Their tears are a soothing balm for One rejected. Their cries, their moans, their utter mourning is collected in My Heart as precious gems for My Crown of Salvation. These are the women of faith in every generation of the Church that await the new Heavenly Jerusalem. See My priest sons, in these holy women of faith, as the holy women who gather about the ministry of My priests in every age. Are they not your comfort in this tiring work of ministering to souls? See how they spend themselves so, attending to Christ's priests. They look to your every spiritual and material need. There can at times even be a competition for your attention. My sons come to all of these women of the Gospel as the image of Christ. With paternal care, care for them as your own daughters; train them in holy wisdom. As humble sons, listen to their holy promptings. See how they might further your ministry, making your manly hearts more sensitive to the promptings of the Spirit and the cry of those in need.

My priest sons, be wise and prudent. Keep the affections of the heart pure, always centered in My Love. Imitate your Master who gave His Body completely in service to His Bride, the Church. Be imitators of My chastity. Be noble in your affection! Take nothing for yourself. Do not grieve the Heart of the Good Shepherd. See in the holy women of Jerusalem, the gift for and the fruit of your priestly ministry. These holy women, the soul of the Church and holy families, are in place to assist Christ's ministers. Bless them, encourage them, give counsel for their family and protect their children. Never be a cause for their weeping by scandal or injustice.

Be tender priests, courageous priests who pause on their way to Calvary to give comfort and aid to these holy women and to receive their presence as a holy balm for the wounds of your own priesthood.

Evan, let us continue this way again soon.

My Lord, Your servant waits upon Your bidding. Bless You, Christ, my Eternal High Priest.

April 8, 2004 – Holy Thursday - **All has been Prepared**

Lord Jesus, Giver of my priesthood, now more than ever am I thankful for this inestimable gift of my priesthood. It is such an honor for me to share in Your Office! There is such beauty in Your Priesthood! Its mystery is caught up in the Eucharist, Penance, Marriage, Baptism, Confirmation, Anointing, and above all the Cross, the fount of all Sacraments. I am wedded to the Immaculate Bride, the Church; may I serve Her with a holy and chaste priesthood and with the fecundity of one who is consecrated in the Spirit! May I be a holy priest to woo souls to the Eternal Beloved. May I be a priest overflowing with charisms of the Holy Spirit to give strength and hope to a people, a flock that is scattered in barren dry fields. Jesus, may I simply be Your Priestly presence.

This morning during prayer I received a series of images: lambs being tethered, staked and slaughtered in the Temple Courtyard; the slaughtered lambs' blood running heavily through the streets of Jerusalem; a cross beam being planed; the Upper Room being swept and dusted; dinnerware being set out at the Table of the Last Supper; Jesus kneeling in solitary prayer with hands outstretched to the Father.

Now this Holy Thursday night I see into the Upper Room. I see Our Lady directing women who are setting out food and drink on a low serving table. This table is adjacent to the end of a low, long horseshoe-shape table. When the room is clear, I see Mary kneel at the setting place for Jesus. I see her eyes darkened already by her anticipatory tears. She prays fervently with arms outstretched begging strength for her Son and His disciple-priests.

I see drape-partitions behind the serving table. Perhaps in this area is where Our Lady will sup with the other disciples? I see through an open window out onto the ancient city of Jerusalem. It is dusk. I then see our Lady standing by the top of the stairs, which is to the right of the window, as the Apostles and Our Lord ascend into the Upper Room. Mary greets each of them with a holy kiss. As Jesus approaches Our Lady, He removes a shawl from His Head. He embraces His Mother with a tender kiss. As they embrace, both fight back the tears for the sake of the disciples! Mary leaves the room through a drape-partition. Jesus instructs His disciples to recline at table. Jesus is at the curved end of the table.

Jesus speaks: **My priest sons, long have I waited to celebrate this Pasch Meal with My Apostles. All of the preparations have been made. From the first day of My stepping into the waters of the Jordan and the descent of the Holy Spirit to anoint My work, I called men chosen to My side, associated in My Priestly work in a particular form and manner that would set them apart from all of My followers. These men were to be My Apostolic pillars, My priestly mediators of the New and Eternal Covenant.**

I saw the Holy Spirit descend as a radiant Dove on each man that I was to call by name in My priestly service. I chose men who came to Me with sin, imperfections, weakness, vice, and a corruptible nature to be raised up as My ministers of Grace! It is not they who chose Me, but I who chose them by name. These men would accompany Me night and day for three years time. They would be formed through My preaching and instruction. They would marvel in My miracles and My power in Words and Love that would draw endless crowds. I would share with them My power and authority from on High, so that they might continue My work of salvation and reconciliation in My Name to the glory of the Father. Each I would take aside and reveal to them their own nature, its weakness and their potential. I taught them as a father and a mother. I formed them in My Priestly Heart.

And when the time drew near, I revealed to them the Suffering Servant who would reconcile all things to the Father, drawing all to Myself as I was lifted up on High. I spoke to them of the Paraclete who would continue to instruct them in all that I said and did. The Spirit who would reveal to them the Father's Love in the Person of the Eternal Son.

Yes My priest sons, all had been prepared for this Night by their formation in the school of My Priesthood; a priesthood of service, love, truth, and reconciliation to the Father. They would continue My work in Sacrament and ministry of the Word. I would place My seal upon their minds, their lips, their hands, their eyes, their feet and their very souls to be configured to My Priestly human soul. I gave to them My final instruction before their partaking in My own Eternal Priesthood as we reclined at Table. My final instruction was from the intimacies of My Heart. My priest sons, in My Farewell Discourse I reveal to you the depths of My Love for My brother priests and My trust in your gift of self to My Priesthood. You are My co-workers with Me in the Father's Vineyard. Do not be timid My sons! See the gift of your vocation, the blessing and honor bestowed upon you! For I call you by name to share in the reaping of this rich harvest. See, you harvest what you did not plant; you reap what you did not sow! How blessed are My priests! Forever, for all eternity their souls sealed with My own priestly nature. For all ages they are sung as blessed!

My priest sons, long have I awaited to eat this Meal with you! The long days of preparation are complete. You will recline with the Lord of the New and Eternal Covenant and arise as priests of this same Covenant, mediators of the New Kingdom of grace, freedom, and victory! My priest sons, see now the Bread given to you, is it not My own Body? You have spent much time in My company and do you not recognize My Presence? See the Cup I offer to you, the Cup of Salvation. Do you not also recognize My Blood, My gift that will poured out for all, so that the hearts of the children may be reconciled to the Father. My priest sons, you know that I can give no more of Myself for the life of the World. In the Eucharist is My all. I ask you then my priest sons, what more can you give to your children? I am your all!

And so I ask you My priest sons, to be truly ministers of My New and Eternal Covenant! Attend to these Sacred Mysteries with every noble desire! Come to My Altar of Sacrifice with the preparation of the Christ. Have you embraced sweetly the Cross that Angels have presented to you daily, in imitation of your Master? Have you immersed yourself into a life of prayer to the Father so to know the very Mind of God? How can you be an effective minister of these Sacred Mysteries if you yourself are not fed from the wellspring of grace and transforming union?

My sons, have you come to the Prisoner of Love with hearts surrendered and with mind and soul attentive, ready to receive from My Eucharistic Heart? Only in this way, in keeping company with your Eucharistic Lord, in adoring My True Presence, can you then possess the faith and cry of recognition as you hold aloft My Body and Blood at the Altar. Do you My sons, recognize your Master who at the Last Supper presented His Body, His Blood for His priests to now take, receive, and eat?

My sons, be transformed by My Priestly Heart. Take and receive. I give it up for you, so that Our Hearts might become one. How I am loved by My sons, when your hearts indeed cry out in recognition in the Eucharistic species of Jesus whom you love! My sons, know that my People of Faith are attentive to the Sacred Mysteries and to their priests. They can see in a priest, one who lives these Sacred Mysteries and one who only speaks the words from a heart, a well that has run dry! My sons, why live such an impoverished priesthood? Your freedoms apart from Me only bring desolation, yes? Your only joy and happiness in your priesthood is to live it from My Priestly Heart. Here you will be built up in your priesthood to be one who is holy and an effective minister of My Grace, for the People of the New Covenant will look upon you and see plainly Jesus whom they love. Theirs will be a cry of recognition of the Christ-Priest in you! My priest sons become as My Eucharistic Presence; let them recognize My Presence in you as My ministers!

When you do this, you do it in memory of Me. You make My Love present as a living testimony and you re-member My Body, the Church. My sons, at the Last Supper, you are now My priests. See now, I lead you to Gethsemane. Do not let your sadness, your weariness deprive you of keeping vigil with Me! Stay awake with Me, your Prisoner of Love. I love you. Will you not stay with Me one hour? Jesus

My Lord, my love compels me to be with You for more than an hour. I hunger for all eternity to be in Your Presence! Your Eucharist is our pledge of future glory! Thank you for this beautiful word for Your priests!

April 9, 2004 – Good Friday Morning – **The Nuptial Embrace**

Come now Holy Spirit; speak to me of the Love of the Father for the Son and the Love of the Son for the Father on this path to Calvary's Mount and from this Tree of Life. Speak to me of Their Love of souls! I will to be configured like the Suffering Servant as one who for You, Father, is despised, rejected, the object of suspicion, scorn, and hatred. But above all I will to be one who loves as Christ loves. And I will that my love might be perfected in the suffering of my own cross. May this love be the fruit of my transforming union with Jesus.

Jesus speaks: **My priest son, let us finish our path to Calvary. How the enemy sorely presses upon Me! My Body is riddled with wounds; every pore is soaked in excruciating pain. My limbs are spent. I have given My all upon this Path. The Father can ask for no more, for I have nothing left to give but My Death! I am near to Calvary's Mount and the Roman guards now hunger for My crucifixion, My final public humiliation! They can see that I can be driven no further. I lay prostrate upon the cool stone; My warm Blood fills its crevices. I fight against the final sleep. After bitter discussion they press into service a stranger, one who is to lift My burden, Simon the Cyrenean. I feel the weight of the Cross being lifted from My back. I can now breathe freely, yet My ribs are bruised, my skin upon My chest is shredded; each full breath is agony!**

I am lifted to My feet by the kindness of My soldier. I lean upon Simon as he bears My load. I take My final steps to Calvary's Mount! The paved stone footing is now gone. I slip upon the fine gravel of the hillside; my feet are slipping from My Blood. Simon holds Me in his strong embrace. This Simon, a stranger, pressed into service, has been pierced in Mercy by One so marred beyond the appearance of Man. His mercy becomes My strength. His strong arm, his strong back

of charity bring Me to My Altar of Sacrifice!

My son, with great joy and tears I have brought My feet to stand upon Calvary's Mount. The Victory is now assured. My final surrender is imminent. Now I am to be wedded to My Bride, our nuptial embrace upon this hard bed of coarse wood.

I receive an image of Jesus taking His first steps as a toddler from Mary's embrace to Joseph, His Guardian.

From My first faltering steps from the embrace of My Mother's Womb, every step of mine was an obedient procession to the embrace of the Heavenly Father's will at Calvary; this holiest of Mounts at which the Son of Man is to be raised up and surrender Himself to the Father's embrace! Father, I return to You! I have prayed and longed to accomplish Your will in all things. Now receive Me Father! And I beg You, Father, to receive My Bride into Your House. I have espoused Her in My Love poured out as Blood. See, She is pure, a spotless Virgin Bride. Purified. Holy. Her womb of Baptismal waters to bring forth children of Your own Household, children of Your inheritance!

Father, I surrender now to the wounds of My Love by which My Love for My Bride is perfected. See, I will give Her Life. I will feed Her with the finest Wheat and Drink of the choicest Vine.

Let us finish it!

Good Friday Evening – **The Tree of Life**

O my Jesus, from Calvary's mount I can see across all of the Earth and I see great legions of the shadows of darkness stream towards Calvary. I see Death, Jezebel, Powers and Principalities. I see the great Red Dragon himself spanning the skies above all his minions.

All of these fallen Angels, a third of Heaven, have been compelled to this Mount. They are desirous to gloat over such shame, the delicious satire for the Son of Man to be crucified. Jesus, here they will be vanquished, yes?

I now receive an image of Jesus being stripped and surrendering His limbs.

Jesus speaks: **Evan, see Me as a frail reed in the breeze upon Calvary. Though barely able to stand from waves of pain racking My Body to and fro, I see Satan's legions closing in. All is in the Father's Plan; their rebellion ends this Day. No longer will they be lords of this material world; they will be vanquished to the eternal abyss.**

My attention is drawn now to the Cross that lay before Me; it weds My final submission of Will to the Father. A tree established death, sin and terror; now a tree will establish life, grace and freedom!

The soldiers turn Me roughly and two of them begin to pull the robe from My shoulders. They find it enmeshed with tatters of skin and scabs, so they yank roughly upon it. They open up fresh wounds on My shoulders, back and chest. I shall baptize this Cross anew in My Blood. I stand before the crowds naked as the New Adam; the New Adam who awaits His Bride to be born of His side. My son, here now I surrender to the nails' embrace. I collapse upon the hard wood of the Cross. Here from My sleep, She, the Church, will be born.

Though My human nature cries out for life, I freely choose in Love to surrender My Life and My limbs. I freely lay My left hand upon the beam. I pray now to the Father for strength as a willing Victim, a Lamb led to the slaughter. The executioner kneels roughly upon My forearm and pins My hand with the point of the iron nail, though I would not pull away. I offer Myself freely. I see the hammer raised between Heaven and Earth as the executioner takes careful aim. O My Mother, have strength now! Did not Our gentle Joseph train Me in the use of this tool, to take careful aim upon the head of the nail? See now, the Heavenly Father guides this hammer to score and bind My Incarnate Flesh upon this Table of Sacrifice.

My son, as the nail is driven through My flesh, I do not cry out! I surrender this pain for the embrace of souls! Trembling now, I offer My right hand to the executioner. It comes up short and My arm is lassoed and pulled from its socket by great force. I feel muscles and tendons snap. My shoulder and back are ablaze with stabbing pain. Again the hammer is raised to Heaven. I see in its place, the Cup of Eternal Salvation to be raised until the end of time. They bind My feet together one atop the other. No longer shall these feet walk upon the Earth in their present form. These feet carried the Good News across the land and now they rest upon My greatest pulpit as I preach My greatest sermon.

Tethers are pulled through the iron bands of the Cross and lo, I am raised up with great alacrity. The sudden force of this movement of the Cross drives the nails wider into My flesh. The weight of My Body comes upon this thin nail in My feet. I struggle to inch My way up the Cross and off the blunt nail. And as I do so, the crown of thorns against the Cross digs terribly into the back of My skull. I am a pained Prisoner of Love. My tiniest movement restrained. With My weight sagging forward, I find it difficult to breath and I must lean My head forward so as not to push the crown against the Cross into My flesh. Father, truly I have suffered all at the hands of Man, but Father forgive them for they know not what they do! They are instruments of a higher intelligence and still Father, all things of Your permissive will can be brought to great good.

As I look down now I see My Mother with the Beloved Disciple, Mary Magdalene, and Mary, the wife of Clopas. Peter, the Rock and My other priest-apostles are hidden, but I hear their prayers, their cries of desolation. My priest sons, which one are you? Are you a priest-disciple who comes to Me at Calvary with a youthful heart and under the Mantle of your loving, attentive Mother. Or, do you keep yourself hidden from My Cross? You now know very well, My sons, as I have instructed you from the depth and intimacy of My Priestly Heart, that your priesthood is born in My self-offering beginning at the Eucharistic Table and finished in My death at Calvary. My priest sons, so too your priesthood is born of the Eucharistic Table. Here it is formed; you are formed by the Sacred Mysteries that you celebrate. And from this Altar you, My sons, are to be brought to the Altar of Calvary, for it is one in the same. If your priesthood is not configured to Calvary in your own death to self for your Bride the Church, then your priesthood is dried up. It will bear little fruit for the Kingdom. But if your love is configured to the Priest-Lamb of Christ Crucified, then your Eucharistic love will be boundless. You will bear a great harvest. Come then, My sons, do not fear the Cross! See, it is the gateway to Eternal Life and to a holy, life-giving and joyful priesthood. There can be no other way! All else is of the enemy!

My priest sons of the Sacred Heart see now on this Good Day for all generations I have entrusted you to Our Mother of the Immaculate Heart. Her embrace is My gift to you in a particular way, for she is the Mother of Priests. Will you not surrender to her Motherly embrace and counsel? She is the Seat of Wisdom! Imagine her wisdom as the Spouse of the Holy Spirit. Perfect. Immaculate. Blessed. My priest sons she is yours. But see, you will find her waiting for you here at Calvary, attending to her crucified Priest Son.

In these long hours upon the Cross, I cried out in utter and complete physical, emotional, and spiritual agony for My Father's Presence. Here now in My most weakened state I am deprived of His Presence in My Humanity. My God, My God why have You abandoned Me? At this signal, the enemy's Legions draw nearer to the foot of the Cross; it is their undoing. For here as I exhale My last breath and My side is opened to pour forth Blood and Water, here at this Cross, the enemy shall be subject forever to exile, subject to the God Man, the Lord of Life, and subject to His disciples!

My priest sons, hear the words of Your Savior in His cry of abandonment. My priest sons, recognize in the souls that you minister to, the bruised, crushed, or the dead in spirit. Be compassion! In your priestly-fatherhood bring them to the Savior who brings all to the Father. My sons let your side be opened, your heart pierced, so that starving, desolate souls may drink of your own wellspring; your hearts pierced for love! Imitate your Master who gave of Himself for all! Reject no one that I send to you! See My hidden appearance in the least of your flock, in those who cry out for Mercy! Be mercy! Be priests! Be My reconciliation and be My ambassadors of hope in the promise of Eternal Life. See My holy exchange with the good thief. My holy obedience, My loving surrender brought him to the grace of conversion, to reconciliation with the Father and then I spoke to him the promise of Eternal Life. My sons speak often of Heaven to souls. Raise their sight to that eternal destiny for which they have been created. Prepare souls for that great journey of Hope, till one day they too will hear: Well done good and faithful servant, this day you will be with Me in Paradise!

My priest sons, for many hours I went without drink and nearly half of My Blood was drained from Me. In My final agony, My Body thirsted with such intensity; my tongue cleaved to My mouth. But My thirst for souls was greater still. Since the time of the Fall, the Eternal Three longed for the company of Man, for the glory of our material creation to be with Us and the Angelic Beings of Heaven. It was such a burden of Heaven to have the children of Earth subject to separation in Sheol. But now after millenniums of time, the Gates were soon to be opened as I gave up My Spirit, to descend into Sheol. I, the Champion of Life, would open the Gates to Paradise. All of My Being ached for this supreme action of Mercy. I thirsted for the Final Cup. Do you understand, My priest sons? When I took to drink from the sponge soaked with wine, I would slate My thirst by drinking My own Blood. For My Blood has purchased the Atonement of the exiled children of Eden. The Gates of the Heavenly Eden are opened to them and Heaven's Halls are filled with the children of Man, now the children of the Trinity! Heaven's Thirst has been slated!

Imitate Me, My sons. Let your entire being ache as My own for souls! Let this hunger, this thirst compel you to not count the cost of your Priesthood. See in your every self-offering of your priesthood as gain for the Kingdom of the Redeemed!

Give them a shepherd's care. Pray with Me: "Father, I pray to have not lost a single one that you have entrusted to Me!" (cf Jn 6:39) Thirst for souls, My sons!

My Hour draws to an end. All has been accomplished with the Divine Will; a New Heaven for the Children of Man and a New Earth free of the enemy's dominion. See, I recreate all things anew. I surrendered My Divinity. I emptied (*kenosis*) Myself so that I, the Son of Man, might redeem Man. I surrendered My Will, My Body and now My Spirit. All (will, body, spirit) is to be redeemed at Calvary. Father, into Your Hands I commend My Spirit.

My priest sons, know that as I lovingly surrendered My Spirit to the Father, so I in great trust and vulnerable Love, surrender My Body, My Blood, My Soul, and My very Divinity into your consecrated hands. Safeguard My Eucharistic Gift. Hold as precious, beyond all treasure, the Body of Christ now surrendered into your embrace! Do not allow the familiarity of the morning Sacrifice dull your keen awareness of these Sacred Mysteries. Know whom it is you hold aloft! Believe! As you receive the surrendered Body and Blood, Soul and Divinity of your Master, so you too are to imitate His surrender to the Father. From this Altar of Sacrifice, surrender your all to the Loving embrace of the Father. Know the joy of the Christ who surrendered His Spirit from His Altar of Sacrifice at Calvary.

And now, it is finished. The Kingdom of the Divine Will is established. My priest sons of My Priestly Heart, all that I have shared with you from My Priestly Heart is to bring you to the Kingdom of the Divine Will, to be configured to Christ the Eternal High Priest as an *alter-Christus*. Spread far and wide the Kingdom of the Father through the inestimable gift of your priesthood. My Love for you My priest sons has brought us here to Calvary, where now It is finished. And behold in your priesthood, the Kingdom of the Divine Will continues. Live from My Priestly Heart! Live in accord with the dignity of your noble calling as a Priest of the New and Eternal Covenant. Joyfully live this life of blessed priesthood for the Love of the Blessed Trinity and for the love of beautiful souls, till the day of your own loving surrender, when you may say to your Master with every confident assurance: It is finished!

My priest sons, live in My Love. My priest sons be My Love. Your Divine Master and Eternal High Priest, Jesus Amen, Lord. So be it. Evan

April 23, 2004 - Second Week of Easter -**Espoused with Me upon the Cross**

I am moved by Our Lord's words to St. Pio on suffering: "Beneath this Cross one learns to love and I do not grant this to everyone, but only to those souls who are dearest to Me...Would you not have abandoned Me, if I had not crucified you?...My son, love is recognized in suffering."

My Angel Guardian, be my witness this day. Let Heaven's Herald behold that I choose to love Jesus and desire that my love might be perfected through suffering. Charity demands it! I desired to be swallowed up wholly by poverty! Let every self-love, every false-love, every disordered thing be stripped away such that I would give myself purely and joyfully to Him who is Love itself.

I now receive an image of Jesus knocking upon the door of a beautiful home in San Marino, CA and inside was a woman of my youth whom I once believed that I loved. But I did not know love. It is the home that I had dreamed of as our own one day. But as Jesus knocked on the door, I stood in the street in the beggar robes of St. Francis. I called to Jesus and He smiled with warmth and came to embrace me. I have met Jesus not in the dreams for my life, but in His desire for my life! My Lord how many countless times you have desired to strip me of everything. May Evan live no longer for himself but only for Jesus!

I hear Jesus speak to me from the Cross: **My good son, how I delight in your self-emptying and in your desire to love your**

Master through suffering and rejection. Is this not the truest test of Love? What is love if it knows only comfort and joy, surrounded by goodness and feasting? It becomes fattened upon pampering and it will not endure the slightest trials that beset it. But such wondrous love is one that would desire no consolation! No sweet comfort! No gift! Save only for the object of their love, their Beloved Himself! My dear soul, see I draw you into My embrace of Love. Will you recognize My Presence in the midst of deprivation and desolation? Will you still cry out, My Beloved is mine and I am His? Yes My son, see I have by My Spirit placed this holy desire for suffering, your love of the Cross and the Sacred Wounds of Love in your heart so that your love might be refined in the white-hot fire of holy desire! If I cool this fire too soon the blade will not be as strong, it would not be as true, and it cannot cut so deeply. And so I intensify the fire of desire that you might become a living flame, an unquenchable fire for union with your Beloved.

Come freely to Me. Come to Me freely as I hang upon the Cross awaiting your company. Will you not keep Me company? Will you not make your love vulnerable for My sake? Will you not bare your chest to Me so that I might pierce your heart by My holy touch?

Yes, Lord!

My son, come, surrender to My touch. Be espoused with Me upon the Cross. Here our wills may become one, our love one, and indeed your very body with My own Eucharistic Body as one. Upon this Cross, here we are espoused in glory to the Father.

My son, be comfort for your Beloved. Grow in sanctity. Do not doubt or be fearful when I as through the Exodus, strengthen and purify your love. For behold, I Am always before you. Be My minister of grace. Remain emptied so that I might fill My priest-servant with holy gifts for My Church, My Bride.

I embrace you sweetly. Trust in Me! Your Beloved, Jesus
Yes, Jesus I trust in You! Your beloved, Evan
Jesus, what is Your Will in regard to these messages I have received

during this Lent for Your priests?

I hear Jesus say: **Let them be disseminated.**
When?

I hear Jesus say: **Sooner than later.**
May Your Divine Will be fulfilled, my Divine Master.

May 6, 2004 – Fourth Week of Easter - **Place My Mark upon My Little Ones**

The Eternal Father speaks: **Behold My son, Evan, I write now upon the canvas of your eternal soul, My eternal plan for your existence, your life as My child. See, I raised you up so that you might be My obedient and faithful servant in My Court. From dawn until dusk, even in your slumber, I call you into a holy dedication to be attentive to the matters of your Heavenly Father's Kingdom. Be solicitous of the Good and Sacred Heart of the Eternal Son. Be vigilant, waiting upon His voice, the call to you as one sent in His Name for the glory of the Eternal Father. Remain confident and steadfast in His service, counting it as treasure beyond all cost to serve as one elect in His Name in the robes of His holy Priesthood. Eternal merit! Eternal glory! Eternal privilege and rank!**

For the servant of the servants there can be no higher gift than to share in the burden of the Heart of the Good Shepherd, to shepherd children of the Father into the embrace of their Good Father! Such honor for such a holy duty! My son, bestow upon My flock My Fatherly blessing of order, peace, holy submission, obedience, and a thirst for the waters of the eternal spring that is holiness. My son, place My mark upon My little ones. Seal their bodies and souls by the mark of the Trinity. Increase the sheepfold. Widen the gate. Reach out your shepherd's staff. Give out the call far and wide. Come to Me,

My children lost, forsaken, hungry, and deprived of all that is good and holy. Feast upon a sumptuous faire. Be fattened in My Goodness. Under My Hand, under the Shepherd's care of the Eternal Son you shall not perish. Come, My children, enter, be submissive to the Thrice Holy One.

My son, do you feel the stirring in your heart of the Good Shepherd? Does the thirst for the souls of My little lambs, for their safety amongst the preying grasp of the enemy, for their resting safely in My pasture, does not this holy desire in your heart burn? Be consumed by this desire My priest son. Forget self and remember only the cost of your salvation. See the Blood of My son come down from the Cross to cover My lambs. By His Blood all has been purchased, wrestled from the hands of eternal death. Let not your care suffer this fate again, as the Good Shepherd wrestled My little lambs from the enemy's embrace. Deliver them My son! My authority is given unto you. Speak in My Name, cast the enemy out of the sheepfold. Be not timid or doubting. Be strong in My Spirit. Be a good shepherd. Victorious is the Lamb! Be a victorious shepherd, a victorious lamb, My priest son. Do not forget your dignity for a moment! It is Heaven's gift and your burden and gift, to share in the Heart of the Good Shepherd!

Eternal Father I thank You and bless You. May the Priestly Heart of the Redeemer be glorified, praised and above all loved by Your priest sons. May our hearts burn with a holy zeal to shepherd Your little lambs safely into Your Eternal embrace.

July 26, 2004 – Be restored in My Love

All day I have been working on a final draft of this manuscript. I am experiencing great retaliation from the enemy. Also I am suffering the intercessory charism of an invisible crown of thorns for the publishing and distribution of this manuscript. I am buckled over in pain from this charism that is but a small portion of one aspect of Our Lord's most profound Passion! I am overwhelmed once again at the depth and measure of His most perfect Love, given to the last drop of His Sacred Blood.

Jesus speaks: **My dear priest son, I see you diligently preparing the recorded pages of the conversation of My Heart and your own. It pleases Me that you now move forward in obedience to the prompting of the Holy Spirit in My regard. It is My most ardent desire to speak to the parched souls of My poor priest sons. How great is My desire to minister to their priestly needs! Only I, the Eternal High Priest of the Eternal Father, can bind and heal the wounds of My priest sons. Day and night I see My priest sons suffer the agonies of doubt, despair, loneliness and isolation, impurity, confusion, every form of weakness, corruption and compromise. I cry out to them, My beloved sons, for whom My Heart is rendered!**

Evan, I desire that the sentiments of My Heart, My most ardent Love and pained sorrow, should be made manifest for their (priests) knowing. I ask you to be My little intercessor on My behalf. Speak upon these pages the gift of My Love, My choicest Love, for My priest sons; My priests sons who are My representatives, who are Me, here upon this Earth. In My Person they act, in My Name they speak, in My Redemption they proclaim, but will they live in My Love? Will they live their priesthood from the Priestly Heart of the Redeemer?

To My priest sons inactive, fallen, compromised by the world, deadened by sin and addiction, weakened by impurity,

dried up without prayer, timid and ineffective without the power of the Holy Spirit, to ALL My priest sons, I beckon!

(I am overwhelmed by Jesus' sadness and longing. Jesus, My sweet Prince, let me bring the balm of consolation to Your wound, the wound of the ordained.)

My Heart wound cannot be contained in your regard, My priest sons. How I long to pour forth My elixir of mercy, My Sacred Blood, upon the wounds of your priesthood. I come to you to restore your priesthood into one of My own making. I, Christ, the One Eternal High Priest, give forth the command that ALL of your priesthood is to be configured most intimately and perfectly with My own. This gift, your office, is not your own possession, it is a sacred trust shared with you by My Eternal Father. For you, My priests, are to be Me to My people. To no one else is My priesthood to be configured; not to yourself, not to a human gospel, not to false doctrine, not to this world, nor to the corruption of sin and death.

My little priest sons, be restored in My Love so that the Church may be restored from the gift of your purified, healed, and divinized love. Know, My priest sons, I desire your healing and conversion. Will you not grant Me access to your broken and emptied hearts? Will you not let Me revive you with My Spirit? I speak to you tenderly because My Love for you is tender. Remember the tenderness of My first call to you for priesthood. I am most desirous to restore the tender intimacies of our conversations. Will you not draw close to Me in ample time set aside for prayer? Choose the better portion like the Magdalene. Be seated at the feet of the Divine Master and provide your own heart as the place of most hospitable welcome. I will come to you.

Be restored, My priest sons. Behold, I bestow upon you great graces during these days, graces of conversion and renewal. Be converted from sin; be sanctified in My Spirit. Behold, I who make all things new, I am doing something wonderful in My Priesthood! Come Spirit of Pentecost. I breathe the Holy Spirit upon My priest sons. Receive the Holy Spirit!

I do love you My brothers with an insatiable Love. Your

Jesus

My Beloved, I thank You and bless You. May Your Love be glorified in Your priests! Evan

October 8, 2004 – The Champion of Divine Mercy

I receive now a most overwhelming vision. Our Lady, O so noble a Mother, kneels before her crucified Son at the moment of His death at Calvary. A shockingly brilliant white light that I understand to be Our Lord descends from the Cross like lightning into the netherworld. I wonder does she witness Jesus' descent into Hell? A cry then comes forth from the Lady of All Sorrows; it is the culmination of all creation, spiritual and corporeal, that mourns the death of its Creator. But this cry of sorrow is permeated with the gift of Divine Mercy. From Psalm 100: "Cry out with joy to the Lord, all the earth. Serve the Lord with gladness. Come before him, singing for joy. Know that he, the Lord, is God. He made us, we belong to him; we are his people, the sheep of his flock. Go within his gates, giving thanks. Enter his courts with songs of praise. Give thanks to him and bless his name. Indeed how good is the Lord, *eternal his merciful love.* He is faithful from age to age."

I am given to understand of Mary as the *Champion of Divine Mercy* for she, the pride of all of God's creation both corporeal and spiritual, is Immaculately conceived through the anticipatory merits of her Son's Mercy. She, who is without sin, of all creation finds His Mercy most precious! His merciful Love is her all. This mystery is beyond our speech. She, who is without stain, in perfect humility knows the free gift of Mercy for her anticipatory redemption. She, like her Son, is one with the sinner! She stands with all as one who has shared in this gift of His Mercy. She is the first and the greatest recipient of His Mercy!

Jesus speaks: **Evan, My priest sons and brothers: How good** it is to receive a precious gem of the Immaculate Heart of the Mother of the Divine, she who kept all these things hidden and pondered them in her heart. How radiant the gem now purified, sanctified in the heart of the Miriam, she who is indeed, the *first* and *greatest* recipient of My Mercy.

She is the *Stabat Mater* who stands as the Champion at Calvary as her Captain, the Captain born of her Immaculate Womb, gives His life for the victory of earth's children. She, by her tears born both of a mother's truest love and of one redeemed in greatest measure by My Merciful Redemption, cries out as the perfect vessel as *Mercy's Champion*. She heralds to her children the gift of so noble, so gratuitous a love that has been poured out as Mercy!

My son, My Mother stood at My side as the *first* and *greatest* recipient of My Mercy. My human, most Sacred Heart was most pained to see her suffer in perfection My own crucifixion, for she is the Co-Redemptrix whose hidden-ness of heart is now mirrored in the hidden wounds she suffers in her Immaculate body! Such perfect hidden-ness, such sublime humility to stand as the *Stabat Mater* who is the *Champion of Divine Mercy*! But what comfort to My soul as she stood with Me through the long hours of Calvary. She, who is the perfection of thanksgiving and of the grateful heart of a servant, is the first and greatest to pour forth her eternal gratitude before the fount of Mercy, pierced for the saving bath for mankind. Mercy's bath would cover the fallen family of man. She is the first servant to return and to give thanks!

Her tears of sorrow mix with her tears of gratitude and in this is how My Heart was given the sweetest of balms. In My solitude upon the hard beam at Calvary, her elixir of precious tears caused My Heart, spent, emptied and to be pierced, to cry great tears of consolation; My Mother, she was the sweetest solicitude in My Passion.

Priest sons and brothers, Mary who is the Mother of all priests is most desirous to teach you in the ways of hidden-ness and eternal gratitude, so as to be priests of ministering consolation to My Most Sacred and Pierced Heart.

O Lord, Jesus, how is it that you could call your priests who minister to the wounds of the Body, the Church, to now minister to the Heart of the Church, Your Sacred and Pierced Heart?

Evan, My son, you priests are the embodiment sacramentally of My Priestly Heart here on Earth. You are ministers of the eternal fount of Mercy and Love. This fount is your origin and this eternal fount is your only source to continue as the ministers of the movement of My Heart!

My Heart has been opened, pierced first for you priests! It is a love made most vulnerable, beginning with you My vessels of sacramental grace. Would not, then, your own love, your compassion for My suffering, your passionate desire for My Love be as the sweetest of balms for My Most Sacred Heart burdened under the pressing weight of the sins, indifference, and blasphemies of this present generation. My priest sons have a singular solicitude for My Heart. Our Lady will teach you in this solicitude, for she is the handmaid of Holy Wisdom. And in your solicitude not only will your thirst be quenched, but you shall come to know Me. In My Heart pierced open you shall know My Person. And in your heart-knowledge of My Divine Person, you shall live truly as My sacramental ministers of grace, of My Mercy and Love.

My priest sons and brothers, I have entrusted you to My Mother, the *Champion of Divine Mercy*. Be her good knights, serving under her banner of Mercy. May My eternal Reign of Mercy and Love begin in the hearts of My priests! Serve Mercy and be free! Serve Mercy and be strong! Serve Mercy and love! Your Divine Master, Jesus, the Fount of Mercy

My Lord, truly you bless me. I am and I pray I always will be your servant of gratitude. Evan

From the Heart of the Eternal High Priest

Chapter Two

Discourses

Although the dialogues I have collected for this chapter are more personal in nature, I believe that they can be of consolation and inspiration to the reader.

IC | XC
NI | KA

November 18, 2003 – Listen for the Impulses of My Heart

Jesus, I am sorry for having ignored the impulses of Your Heart. You have made Your Love vulnerable to me, a weak creature. Such mystery! Let me never forget such love! Let me never forget how tender is Your Heart!

I received a word from Our Lady: *My son on the Feast of my Birth I presented to you a gift of my Beloved Heavenly Spouse. As the Holy Spirit overshadowed me at my conception, birth, and the annunciation, the breath of the Spirit too shall overshadow you. As you long to know and love my Immaculate Heart, so shall I lead you to know and love the breath of the Holy Spirit. See His breath recreate you, breathing life into your heart. Your body is to ache with the force of His presence.*

Yes, my son Evan, you good priest, listen attentively to the impulses of my Son Jesus' Heart. See how truly noble is His Love, how kingly; and yet He stoops from the Heavens to speak lovingly to you as His little one. Would you keep your King waiting? Would you cause pain to His Most Sacred Heart? Through my maternal mediation I have presented you before the very golden throne of my Son.

I have an awareness of somehow being present to Christ the King seated upon His golden throne. Our King is wearing white and gold armor that is adorned with blue medallions. Jesus wears a crimson robe. I humbly bow before such Majesty. Speak Lord, Oh noblest of Lords, for your humble servant is listening for Your every Word, Your every impulse, Your every command.

Christ the King now speaks: **Evan, my delightful son. Do you not find Me noble in appearance?**

Oh yes Lord!

I tell you My glory was hidden during my earthly life. I did not win to me souls who craved the trappings of earthly glories; rather it was to be My Love; My Love crucified, My Love vulnerable, My Love sweet to the eternal soul. Joseph you must imitate Me in My Love. You too must remain hidden. Remember, seek only to be pleasing to Our Heavenly Father. This alone suffices! This alone should be your thirst!

I now experience a strong movement of joy in my heart.

You gladden My Heart when you are attentive to the impulses of My Heart. How can I speak with you, how can we sup in one another's company if you do not come to Me? Let your heart become more each day a burning ember of My Love and I will draw through you many to My Company.

I then received an image of Jesus and Mary as King and Queen Mother. Mary stands at Jesus' right hand and she places her hand upon the Good King's right hand and together they give me a benediction. Thank you Mother! Thank you Christ the King, my Beloved Lord.

December 8, 2003 – Feast of the Immaculate Conception –
A Trinitarian Blessing!

On this Feast of Our Lady I am somehow present to the Court of

Heaven. It is Our Lady who brings me to the Thrice Holy One for a blessing upon my priesthood.

The Eternal Father speaks: **My priest son I give you My blessing. I am your Father who has consecrated you from before your birth to serve My People; to wear the priestly robes adorned with Miriam's mystical roses. See she has presented to you her mystical roses for she loves her priest son.**

I receive an image of Our Lady placing a bouquet of roses into my arms. She then embraces me and kisses me upon the cheek. I bow my head for her blessing and she touches my head and gives her blessing. She blesses my lips. She then places her hand upon my heart and her other hand over the Sacred Heart of her Eternal Son. Rays of Light come from her hand to my heart.

The Eternal Father continues: **It is My Chosen Daughter's desire to adorn you with her mystical graces.**

I am being reminded of the many years that I shut myself off to the life of mystical grace.

My son, I bend all things to My most perfect will. See as My Priest son, I now fill your years with service to My People. I draw you into My Garden of mystical grace. Here is your abode. I love you, My priest son, and I bless you for your yes to serve your Father.

I give praise, honor, and glory to you Eternal Father. Your Love sorely humbles me. I am most unworthy, but I know that Your Love suffices for my imperfection. All of the wounds of my heart are healed in Your Heavenly Love. Jesus, the Incarnate Word, my Eternal High Priest, I present myself to You.

I receive an image of Christ the King. He is wearing a crown and is dressed in priestly garb. Jesus the Eternal High Priest incenses me. He lifts His eyes to the Father and intones His priestly prayer before the Father.

Jesus speaks: **Live in My Love, My priest. As I have done, so you must do as to imitate My Love for the Father.**

I receive an image of Jesus drawing nearing to me. He places His forehead to mine and He places His Hands upon my head. He breathes upon me and says: **Receive My Spirit.**

I then see Jesus ascend to the Cross in His priestly garb. Jesus speaks the words: **Do this in memory of Me.**

I do will it, Jesus; I desire to die to myself so that I might live for You!

I then receive an image of the Dove of the Holy Spirit's great white wings hover above me. Come Holy Spirit!

The Holy Spirit speaks: **My priest son, as you are drawn to the Immaculate One, I the Spouse within Her living Temple coo with Love. It delights Me to see you My priest son love the Chosen Daughter. It delights Me that in your love for your Mother, you fill others with confidence for her love. My Mother! My Confidence!** (*Mater mea, Fiducia mea*) **Know My son that from your earliest years, the seeds of loving devotion of Mary were planted before your path.**

I then sense the Holy Spirit lovingly admiring Miriam as a beautiful white rose. The Holy Spirit is the proud gardener admiring the handiwork of His loving care. I see myself being planted in this rose garden of the Spirit. I receive water, pruning, nutrition, and the breath of the Spirit so that I might blossom as a mystical rose for the garments of Our Lady in Heaven.

The Holy Spirit continues: **Trust, Evan, in My gifts, My charisms and the charisms of My Mystical Rose Miriam. You are to recognize by now My presence, My movement within your heart; this the enemy cannot reproduce! Recognize the enemy's movements in your mind: fear, doubt, anxiety, worry, frustration, tension headaches, agitation, blockage, and coldness. Rather, only in the Spirit will your soul find its fire, its warmth, its safety, and the heat to refashion your will. Recognize My movements! Do not fear! Trust, for My Voice is as sweet as the morning Dove in the Garden. Listen for it!**

Holy Spirit, You are the Delightful Lover and the most Welcomed Guest. Come, dwell within me. Find your perch within my heart. Overshadow me.

December 31, 2003 – Eve of the Solemnity of Mary, Mother of God – Surrender Each Day

The Eternal Father speaks: **Evan, My little son, thank you for coming to the Eternal Spring of My Son. Do you wish to become My Eternal Flame?**

Yes, Father, you know that I do.

Then surrender My son. Surrender to the Almighty Power, the Greatness of your God. What can withstand the force of Me? Only a fragile, weak human heart! So great is My love for My children. Each day surrender your heart to Me Joseph. Let yourself fall into the ocean of My Mercy, the embrace of the unknowable abyss of My Love. Abandon yourself to My Providence and care, My little son, and I shall prepare your arm for battle.

Confide all things to your Mother on this eve of her Feast. She, the Mother of God, is your sweet fair Mother. She alone of all My creation has entered and probed the Heart of the Eternal Father. Be obedient then to her instruction. Be her servant. Wait upon her every desire, her every impulse. She most perfectly will bring you to the Son, who alone brings you to the Father.

Yes, Father, I will serve faithfully in my Lady's court all the days of my life.

I bless you, My son, this day in the Name of the Most Holy Trinity. Shalom. Your Father in Heaven

All Glory be the Father, and to the Son, and to the Holy Spirit.

January 8, 2004 – St. Francis is Our Lady's Captain

While in prayer I am reminded to grow in St. Francis' holy imitation of Christ.

I hear Our Lady speak: *Receive the blessing of Francis. He is my captain and he is your captain. How alike unto the Christ. How graced his perfect imitation. Be Christ!*

I receive an image of Francis wearing a gleaming silver chain mail over his brown tattered robes. He is at the head of a vast army. He points his sword and his troops take to the offensive as they move to outflank the enemy. He holds up his arms in cruciform and is in the agony of the stigmata. A vast number of the enemy is vanquished at this terrible sight of the Love of Christ crucified enfleshed in the Seraphic Father Francis!

Francis then turns to me and speaks with great conviction: *Be Christ, Evan! Be Christ!*

I then receive an image of the dawn of a radiant Sun appear over this dark and smoky battlefield. The entire enemy is vanquished! It is springtime.

I hear Jesus speak: **See the things to come. Live vigilant in the expectation of My coming. Let not a day pass that is not surrendered to the glory of the Father and the holy crucible of My Love. This is the life of Francis and this is My Life that I lived for you to imitate. Be caught up in this holy furnace, to be consumed in My Love. Let My Love transform you. Let My Love transfix you to My Holy Cross. Be nailed to My Cross, fixed by a love that is ever steadfast, ever vigilant. Go now in My Peace. Surrender to the Majestic Love of your Good King.** *Pax!* **Jesus**

Bless Your Holy Name Jesus. Bless Your Holy Arrival. Bless Your Sacred Love. I love You, Evan

January 14, 2004 – Trained for Battle

The Blessed Mother speaks: *Evan, my little priest son, be obedient now to the Father's will in all things. So, as you surrender those past years at seminary, darkened by the enemy, know that I was always present to you. I your Mother, Salve Regina, listened to your pleas and took all things to My Sorrowful and Immaculate Heart. My son, you were being trained for battle. As a new soldier often does not understand the merit of their training, so you too were being trained by your Captain. You were learning the craft and tactics of the enemy: the strength of his resolve, the depth of his cunning, and his infiltration into the very heart of the Church. You were brought to desolation so as to know that in this battle ALL depends upon the strong arm of the Most High. All depends upon the Holy Eucharist that alone strengthens My foot soldiers. All depends upon prayer, intimacy with the Eternal Father so that His Love reaches you from the Highest Heaven. All depends upon your sweet consecration to the Heart of your Master. In a most perfect docility is the Lord free to act in Power. For the Woman clothed in the Sun has been chosen* (by her docility) *and appointed by the Most High to crush the head of the Serpent.*

My son, hold tightly to the promise of the Covenant. You are never forsaken! You are forever held dear in the embrace of your Mother. Let your Mother instruct you all of your days in the holy school of Nazareth. Let humility be your sweet virtue; then, you will know the secret of Nazareth. In **humility** *is learned docility. In* **docility** *is learned the gentle voice of the Spirit. In the gentle* **voice** *of the Spirit is learned the Heart of the Son. And in the* **Heart** *of the Son is learned the will of the Father. In the* **will** *of the Father is learned* **Love**. *Be humble my son.* **Be Love!** *Your Mother embraces you sweetly and smiles upon you. I cover you with my Mantle of Heaven and I kiss your forehead with my lips that speak* *to you. Shalom, Evan!*

Ave Maria! Good and gentle Mother your love pierces my heart. How you have loved me in ways hidden and lost as I stumbled in darkness. For these difficult years in seminary, let your song of Motherly affection illumine your path to me and strengthen my consecrated love to you.

January 29, 2004 – Free to Love

I received an interior image of myself before the Cross and Jesus bent down to present to me a lighted sacred taper.

Jesus speaks: **Come then, Evan, do you desire to be a flame of My Eternal Love?**

I do desire it Lord! I will it. I then see myself being handed the lighted taper from Jesus.

Then be enflamed by My Love. Be fire! Be the fiery light of My Love to hearts that are saddened and filled with darkness. Be then free to love. Free to love with Heaven's fire! Be set ablaze! Only My purifying fire can destroy those remaining vestiges of desire for honor, riches, timidity, self-awareness, anger, and un-forgiveness. Care not what your brothers think, care only of the Father's glorious will! Imitate Me in My abandonment. I cared not for human honor or respect. These are imperfect and false. I cared only to love the Father's will in complete joyful surrender. Rediscover this joy! My son, surrender to the complete freedom of docility. What worry could one have when compared to the embrace of the Father's Love. I tell you, you are blessed by My Father in Heaven. You are known and you are loved.

Put aside anxious thoughts and keep company in your Father's House. Attend here in heart, mind, and soul. In this will your heart remain singular. My son, receive My sweet

Peace! You wonder how you could ever be as a saint on earth? I tell you Francis himself smiles upon his son. He helps to train your heart for the crucible of Love. Will you walk the martyrs' steps? Will you walk to the gibbet? Do you desire My Fire? Be free to love. Free to give. Free to receive. Ponder these things in your heart, My son. Your Savior-Redeemer, Jesus

February 12, 2004 – I Thirst for Love

As I meditate upon the crucifix, I hear Jesus speak to me interiorly in a raspy, weak voice.

Evan, Evan, My son, I thirst for your love. Upon the altar of My sacrificial love I await your company. Will you keep company with your Beloved? I share now with you from the Heart of your Eternal High Priest. How long, lonely, and fiercely painful were my three hours upon Calvary's Mount. I the Eternal Word who spoke into being All of Creation by the Father's creative love now stood naked, stripped of everything, of My Divinity, My noble birth, My power. Save for My Mother, the Co-Redemptrix, John, My beloved priest, and Mary Magdalene, My apostle of purified love, My loneliness, My abandonment would have been unbearable even for the King of Kings. My human heart by My own Divine Hands was created for Love, for holy companionship, for blessed communion amongst the children of Earth, the children of the Father.

I have fashioned your heart in the same fashion; a priestly heart that longs to reconcile My People to the Father's endless Mercy. A priestly heart that for Love's sake is impelled as my own to climb Calvary's Mount to be stripped of all, to be made vulnerable for Love's sake. My son, become as sifted ground wheat, as the fruit of the vine. Ripened under the light of the noon sun, sweetened, harvested in due season and crushed for its tender elixir. Be made vulnerable in your priesthood for the sake of Love. A libation to be poured out upon My thirsty children. My son, give from your heart, your grace overflowing, and give unto the last drop. Then I may fill you again and again with the choicest, most lavish portion. "I will lavish choice portions upon the priests and my people shall be filled with My blessings says the Lord" (Jeremiah 31:14).

My priest son, see I train your strong arm for battle against the powers of death and darkness. Know that the enemy retaliates with mortal force. Remain covered in My precious blood, adorned in our Lady's garments of purity and humility. The enemy cannot penetrate such armor of Light. In this he is defeated. But do not underestimate his cunning and cruelty. Always be vigilant. Test all things. Try all things by the standard of Love that is the Holy Cross. In this the victory is given over the enemy for all eternity.

See I have strengthened and blessed the company of My priest son. I have blessed you with companions of my own choosing. I have done this for the sake of your Mother's love and mercy. She attends to her priest son with tender, tender, sweet maternal solicitude. She rejoices in her little priest son, yes? Please her in all things! Listen to her instruction. She teaches you in the manner of the Eternal High Priest. Wait upon every bidding of the Handmaid of the Lord. Delight in fulfilling her desires with greater and greater love and alacrity.

I receive an image of Jesus the King of Kings and Mary Queen of Heaven and Earth being seated in their thrones, side by side. He holds her hand and they both gently smile upon me. They speak together: **Be consecrated in our united Sacred and Immaculate Hearts. My son, live your priesthood in the blessing of the Most Holy Trinity.**

I then see an image of Jesus placing His hand over Mary's and together they bless me in the Name of the Most Holy Trinity.

Your Mother loves you. Your Lord Jesus strengthens your priesthood this day.

March 2, 2004 – Hour of Mercy

I have wrestled with spiritual sloth this day and now this evening I have asked Jesus to illumine for my understanding the physical suffering that I endure most every day at around the three o'clock Hour of Mercy. Since 1995, I have suffered from a neuro-cardio condition that results in vertigo and great fatigue.

Jesus, behold the canvas of my soul; write upon these blank pages of my journal so that I may drink fully of Your exquisite Love! Your Love is an exquisite Feast!

Jesus speaks: **My son, it has taken some hours to rouse you from your spiritual slumber. Be vigilant, Evan! The enemy's onslaught is hidden, but vicious, yes? You have asked me of your hour of suffering. Know that this is a gift from Me! Throughout these years, I have through this debilitating suffering called you into the depths of My Passion. I have called you to meditate through your weakness, the ever-present call to surrender yourself more fully into My abandonment. I allow this suffering that you experience so that you might be brought more fully into My abandonment to the Father. In this you will be more perfectly configured to My Person. My son, as an immolated offering to the Father let your sweet fragrance rise unto Heaven. During your hour with Me know that My Mercy is very present. Release every ounce of suffering into My embrace. I will make it sweet. I will make it meritorious so that you may be a channel of grace through your priesthood. Invite the Mother of your heart to be with you. Speak to your Guardian and your friends of Heaven. Make this hour your best hour of prayer, aside from the Holy Mass. Let yourself rest in My Mercy. Let your body be pierced for Love's sake. Evan we will continue this conversation.**

March 17, 2004 – Feast of St. Patrick - **Train Each Day**

Jesus, why is such grace given to me a sinner! Yesterday I failed over and over! It was as if no charity could pass through my lips. I turned aside any desire to be in Your company. I am a sinner. Please leave me, a wretched betrayer of Your Mercy and Love. I cannot stand to be near You! I am only a worm, less than a worm! For I have received Your grace and I have refused cooperation with it. Jesus, cover me in Your Precious Blood. Forgive me! I am nothing without You! Erase my existence if I do not live in You. Have Mercy, Jesus. Mother Mary, my instructor, I beg your pardon. I expect no comfort, only discipline! I beg only to be used for your humblest tasks!

Mary speaks*: Evan, listen to the heart of your Mother. My gentle son, do not let your spirit become discouraged too deeply; this is of the enemy. Know that the Hearts of Union, your Master and your Mother, withhold not our love, our tenderness, our mercy, our compassion. Know that all things can be used to build up the Kingdom within you. Train your ear, train your tongue, discipline your body, and guard your senses. Become a tower of purity and righteousness and goodness as my own spouse, St. Joseph.*

See I enfold you in my mantle, my refuge for sinners. I guard you from the enemy who targeted you for destruction! Destruction! Your old ways must cease! Old habits, old comforts and laxity will only bring your downfall. The enemy will not stop his onslaught. You cannot go this alone and in ignorance of the traps that beset you. Forget not the lesson of the saints. Though they may have stumbled, their hearts were given over to become an ardent furnace of charity; apostles of love even for their enemies, those who sought their destruction!

My son, tighten your belt, roll up your sleeves, exercise your heart in charity. Train each day my son. Let not a day be wasted,

nor a forfeit of grace. *Do not settle for the former pleasures. They
are empty foolishness in the light of what is presented to you: a
crown of victory, a crown of love, and a crown of suffering! Aim
high, Evan, and keep your eye on the prize! Do not falter in disbelief. Know that you are an elected vessel for greater things, to
bring glory to the Father's Kingdom. Come now, take cheer. You
have many intercessors, friends in Heaven who pray for you before
the Throne of the Thrice Holy One. Surrender to their mediation
and the enemy will be conquered each day in your limbs and in
your lips and in your heart and mind! Forget not the daily prayer
of my beads and the Wedding Feast of the Lamb. These are your
armor, your gateway to grace from on High.*

*My priest son, surrender to the grace of this appointed Lent.
My Son reveals the depth of His Priestly Heart to you! What could
compare, what could compete with such intimacy? Surrender and
present to your Mother a beautiful bouquet of Love that will comfort
my most Sorrowful Heart; my heart pierced in agony and love for
the cost of our Redemption by my beloved Son! Share His Priestly
Heart, Evan. Let them know His Heart as I do, their Priest-Shep-
herd-Victim of Love. Evan, be reconciled to the Father. I bless you
and send you forth in the blessing of the Most Holy Trinity. Your
Advocate, Mother Mary*

Mother, I am deeply touched by your solicitude. I surrender
to your mediation. Mother, refashion me anew into the image of
your Son! I love you and thank you. Your son, Evan

May 7, 2004 – Leaping Lambs

Jesus speaks: **Evan, come to My Sacred Heart. Feel its beat
echo with your name, with the delight of Your Savior in His
little priest son. Evan, attend to Me now. Keep vigil with Me
the Good Shepherd as we guard over the sheepfold, the lambs**

of My Father's embrace. Be still, listen and watch. Be keenly aware of the enemy's movements within the shadows. Recognize the traces of his hidden movements. Outflank his cunning. Meet him at his attack. Drive him back by the standard of My staff-cross.

My son, begin with your own vigilance. You are the target of incessant attacks. See this for what it is, Evan, your purgation and resulting purification. If the enemy finds a weak link, then this link is to be removed and repaired, stronger than before. Thus your own flesh becomes a living armor impenetrable from the biting wounds of the enemy. His claws cannot pierce your flesh. Only My darts of love will wound you! You are as pierced through to the heart by the thrust of My Love. Does not your body writhe in pain from the force and fire of this Love?

Yes, Lord!

Be purified by My Love's embrace. Become aglow with its pulse. Become as a living ember free of all imperfection by the strength of the flame. Set ablaze My lambs with this fire of Love; let them leap into its burning embrace.

I receive an image of lambs leaping into the Sacred Heart to be consumed by this Divine Fire of Love.

Be benevolence and love for the lambs. Be a paternal heart that corrects and reproves with every gentleness and solicitude for the soul. Be untiring patience and constant in your care. Love them as I have seized your heart in the grasp of My embrace. Few know of this love in such intimacy, but many are to see this love in the heart of My elect shepherds.

Jesus, I desire to be that good shepherd. Assist me! I am so often frozen by timidity and ineffectiveness. My mind, body, and heart become sluggish. I walk so often in darkness. I desire Your presence and the Counsel of Your Spirit. Jesus, I will to be Your Good Shepherd. Train me in this holy duty, Divine Master. Form me! I receive an image of me as a young boy standing next to a very tall Jesus in a shepherd's robe with staff. He teaches me to be attentive to the needs of the sheep, so as to have a shepherd's sight. I then see myself meeting the Holy Father and I take his hand to my heart to impart to me his charism of the good shepherd. Jesus, my Good Shepherd, I ask you now to place your hand upon my heart and impart to me a share of Your love, the source of every Good Shepherd.

Jesus is there a word to share with my brother Luke?

Luke my brother, trust in your Good Shepherd. My son as I left My sweet home in Nazareth did I not leave behind Me not only a life of gentle comfort and the sweet bliss of My Mother's daily company, but also I faced the desert of exile. For forty days and forty nights like the Israelites of old the Spirit would lead me so that My trust perfected, I would be as a perfectly toned instrument to receive every chord of the Father's direction. I set out alone stripped of all my former life so that I might be born anew as through the fire of abandonment. Here removed of possessions and safety in comforts the human is stripped to the nakedness of one emptied before their Creator. They return to a state of the womb so that they now might be refashioned in spirit! My son, become the spiritual man! It is not the natural man that endures but the spiritual man unto eternity. Every saint has come this way before to be stripped of the old self, to be naked in vulnerability to become clothed in the garments of immortality, holiness and righteousness!

My son, can you pack all of your things for this desert trek to where the Spirit is leading you? Come light of foot and journey far, far into the heart of the desert. Here the Spirit can move you with freedom by docility and trust. I left Nazareth and a widowed Mother to hear the voice of the Spirit who called to Me, the Spirit who echoed the Song of the Father's Love. Hear this song, Luke and run to the Father. Delight in His call to you. I love you Luke. Come follow Me! Jesus, once of Nazareth

Bless Your goodness, Jesus! Bless Your Name forever!

May 13, 2004 – Feast of Our Lady of Fatima - **Be Attentive to the Handmaid of the Lord**

Mother, who so often has appeared to the earth's little children, may I come to you as a little child about your knees. Find me irresistible, My Lady, such that you would never put me down but forever hold me and fondle me upon your lap. I now experience the Blessed Mother's sweet air to fill the room. Miriam! Blessed be Our Lady of Fatima, radiant in heavenly light, whose Immaculate Heart is pierced for her children by their sinfulness, coldness, and indifference to her Son. Mother may my priesthood be for you only a sweet reminder of your Son. Oh, please Mother, let me not grieve your heart in any way. Especially by impurity, pride, selfishness, sloth, and sins against charity.

Mary speaks: *Evan, my gentle priest son, please write. I appear to you with my two spiritual children, Jacinta and Francisco, within the folds of my Mantle. How beautiful their young trusting souls who at great peril and against unlawful authority ran to receive the company, the visit of the Immaculate One. In my great delight in their vulnerable souls, my Son called them early to my embrace. One, Lucia, was to continue for many years as my light to numerous pontificates and generations. Their solicitude for their mother's instructions pulled so tenderly upon my maternal heartstrings. How Yeshua as a young boy would come running earnestly whenever Joseph or I called for Him! He had completely entrusted Himself obediently to our care. As He swiftly would carry out the Heavenly Father's every desire so Jesus attended to our direction and guidance. The Good Shepherd was a good boy! How blessed those years! And in every generation my Son has blessed me with a great multitude of spiritually born children who in imitation of the Holy Child attend to their Mother with all haste and attentiveness. Mother whom they love! What blessings for my Sorrowful Heart so grievously wounded by the sins of men.*

Mother Mary, let me be your errand runner; let me fulfill your every task you would ask of me. Mother, call loudly my name when I am far away from your love, and gently whisper my name lovingly when I have drawn near. May this priest son whom you love bring delight to your heart.

You delight my heart greatly and that of my Eternal Son, when by your preaching and piety draw my children into the folds of my Mantle. For here they can remain safely within my embrace. Evan, my son, may your heart burn with a great joy to wait upon the Handmaid of the Lord.

Yes, my Lady, I count it as pure joy and honor.

My son, then be attentive to your Mother who places her hand upon your priestly heart and imparts to you the blessing she gave unto her own Eternal Son: the prayer of consecration for the Priest, Prophet, and King. Know that my hand remains upon your heart as I direct your heart always in the work of my Son's Kingdom and Vineyard. My wisdom shall fill your speech. Do not be anxious for I am instructing you in all things. My blessing of shalom I give to you this night my priest son of my Immaculate Heart.

Yes Mother! *Ave Maria!* I thank you and I love you. Evan

June 1, 2004 – The Church Needs your Holiness!

Lord Jesus, how I look so fondly upon the graces of Lent that were poured into my soul as dry parched land. I drank fully the abundance of these graces and now, now I can barely recognize or speak of these mystical graces! Jesus, what must I do to be restored to such intimacy? Death to self! Death to Evan, so that the Master might live within me! I pray Lord Jesus to be poured out as a living libation. May the Living Waters of Eternal Life be poured into this now empty vessel so that my soul might drink and others drink from my own heart. Holy Spirit, guide me by Your gift of Counsel so that I might know the path to be restored.

Now while in prayer I receive two images. First, I was holding aloft a sword to Heaven and Christ's rays illumined this sword. Then I received an image of John the Beloved and he was praying with Holy Scripture. He went into ecstasy and from his belly came forth a beautiful golden beam towards Heaven. I now hear from my Guardian Angel: *Be fed upon the Word of God.*

Jesus speaks: **My son, close and keep closed the door of access the enemy has into your heart, your imagination, your energy and focus. My son, have I not laid a rich enough faire before you to feast upon day and night? Do not be distracted by small insignificant things. Have I not created you and infilled you for an infinitely greater purpose?**

Yes, my Master. Please have mercy on your weak servant. Of my own I am too weak, but I find courage in the exhortation of Your Apostle Paul: "I can do all things through Christ who strengthens me." (Philippians 4:13)

My son, do not grow weary of the spiritual life that has been offered to you at great cost. Yes, My Blood as droplets of purchase upon your indebted soul, but also the prayers and sacrifices of the saints on earth and in Heaven. Many sacrifice so that you might be holy! The Church needs your holiness! Do you not see this? Yes, My son, the time is urgent! Souls are being eternally lost each day. Make these souls as your own in the Heart of the Eternal Good Shepherd. Do not discount the power of My grace. I can and will change hearts but I am in need of holy apostles who will not count the personal cost, the death to self, but who will give all for the love of souls! Surrender once again into My embrace and know that solitude and peace of My Company. I will walk with you upon this path to eternity. I never leave your side, but I am drawn to your soul, for here I find the eternal mark of My Father and the sweet odor of My Mother. I hear the gentle beating of the wings of My Spirit Dove.

And so as I come to you and speak to you from the infinite height and reach of My Mercy, say unto Me: "I desire you, My Lord, above all else, above everyone else! Come then Lord

Jesus, come. **Possess my soul; animate me by Your Spirit. Direct my soul in perfected charity to the embrace of the Eternal Father. Come, Lord Jesus, come!** *Maranatha!"* **You remain in My Love. Jesus of Nazareth**

My Sovereign Lord! I am not worthy to be visited, but I am in great need of Your Mercy. Restore Me O Lord. Enkindle my heart, Holy Spirit. Amen. Amen! Evan

June 8, 2004 – The Heart of the Redeemer cannot be restrained!

I am on retreat with my brother priests and I am praying in the Blessed Sacrament chapel. There are brother priests here with me. I am impressed to honor every hour of this retreat with prayer and recollection as so many people are praying and sacrificing for us while we are on retreat. Mother Mary, drape your mantle around your priest sons gathered here. In the Name of your Son deliver us from all evil and step upon the head of the Serpent that is desirous to rob us of the graces of these days. St. Pio, be my heavenly intercessor. Attend to your spiritual son and if it is pleasing to the Eternal Father, may your charisms become present to help rebuild the Church in this new millennium.

Lord Jesus, Your Spirit cries out within me! I desire with insatiable longing to know You, to see You, to hear You, and to speak with You; to be possessed by You and to possess You in this same movement of Love. Holy Spirit, gift of Love to the Son from the Father, fan into flame my desire to be one with My Beloved. Heart of the Redeemer, envelop me, consume me, purify me! I receive an image of the Heart of Jesus coming before me and fitting neatly within my own heart.

Jesus speaks: **My son, my blessed son, it is I, the Heart of the Redeemer, the object of your ardent love. Let us whisper** in hushed tones the intimacies of our Love. I, your Savior and Lord, the Second of Persons of the Most Holy Trinity, with great joy and ever-youthful enthusiasm come to you to be poured out into your heart, to stir up lost sentiments of the holy bond of our Love. Yes My son, you have experienced your heart cooling and drying out, not yet to its center, but the ardent, ever-present desire and love for your Beloved has begun to wane. Was My Love not sufficient? Did your troubles, your cares, and concerns become lessened apart from Me? I tell you do not fear, My little one. Draw close to Me and I run to embrace you in mercy and joy. The Heart of the Redeemer cannot be restrained! See how potent My Love! How vulnerable My Love to wait upon My own creatures. Can you comprehend this mystery? As your love is perfected, the Divine transformative grace of the Most High overshadows you, infills you, recreates you with a Divine movement. You are transformed by this sanctifying grace.

How My Heart trembles with joy and anticipation to see a new creation in my sons and daughters! The miracle of grace is something beautiful to behold for the Heart of the Redeemer. By My yes to the Father's will, I see, cherish and love the new creation of man divinized, raised higher than the Angelic Powers. Oh, if My children only knew the dignity to which they are called. To bring a shrill cry from the Heart of the Redeemer who now possesses the love of His children transformed; love that is now a holy offering to the Eternal Father. A glorious offering!

See My priest sons gathered around Me now? Place your brother priests within the hidden recesses of your heart. My balm of mercy and healing shall flow through you, if you permit it! Surrender, Evan, and be transformed. I give you a great gift of promise. Rejoice!

This is a correction from Jesus, for in truth, as I heard these words from Jesus I was feeling a great sense of burden for such a ministry to the ordained. It is so very difficult for me to minister to brother priests!

Evan, I know your heart better than you know your own. You cannot remain hidden, but surrender every movement and sentiment to My embrace.

See, I give unto you a special heavenly intercessor in Pio. He will take you by the hand upon the dark roads you must travel so that you might come unto the great heights of perfection in your Divine Master. Be not afraid. I go before you. Come follow Me. Again, I say again, surrender and become My living Image in priestly robes. I bless you this day. My son, be stouthearted and love your brother priests. Your Eternal High Priest, Jesus

My Master how sweet is Your voice to be heard in this tired heart of mine. I thank you and bless you. Pio, I am sorry if I am such a burden to you, slow pupil that I am in the school of the Cross. Please be patient with me as the Madonna was with you! Evan

June 13, 2004 – Solemnity of Corpus Christi –
My Tears Mixed with your own this Night

During the Holy Mass at the Liturgy of the Eucharist I was overcome by the power of the Holy Spirit and I began to weep uncontrollably. I found it most difficult to complete the words of institution, as my heart seemed to become one with the Priestly Heart of Jesus from the Cross. I cannot describe the power of His Agape Love from the Cross. All my soul could do was weep. This weeping continued throughout the distribution of Holy Communion. My heart remains sorrowful hours later now as I write this.

I now receive an image of a well-armored Angel above me. He looks up to Heaven. His right arm reaches up to Heaven and his left hand holds a sword pointed to the pages of my prayer journal. The sword drips blood. St. Pio, stay with your priest son this night. I am beset by weakness. I need the love of a brother priest; else I should die from this sorrow!

Jesus speaks: **My beloved priest son, write in your tears. My**

Mercy hears your pierced heart cry out for love of the *Bread come down from Heaven* and for your sadness for the offense and cold indifference to the glory of such a Feast of Love. Evan, do not let your peace be taken from you. I hear your cry, the wrenching of your heart. I know your love for My Heart and you bring Me comfort in My sorrow. You bring a sweet balm of anointing to the Man of Sorrows.

Jesus, why was I so overcome at the consecration with tears from the Holy Spirit?

Need you ask, My son? You are a priest of the Heart of the Good Shepherd. You prayed these words of institution from the very depths of your heart in union with Christ the Eternal High Priest and Good Shepherd. Did not the words from My own lips mix with My tears as I celebrated My last Pasch with My beloved disciples? These are tears of the God-Man who cries out in ardent desire for the hearts of His children. These are the tears of the God-Man who cannot be consoled or comforted as the sons of Adam sin against the gift of Divine Love. These are the tears of the God-Man who weeps from the hardened hearts that are turned away from His own Sacred Heart, pierced for Love and Mercy's sake.

My priest son, how few of My priests truly know the Heart of their Shepherd and Eternal High Priest. My tears mixed with your own this night for the brotherhood of priests. When will they allow Me to tend them, My little priests? When will they allow Me to speak to them intimately from the Heart of the Son of Man, pierced by sorrow and parched for their sweet surrender unto My company?

I begin to weep once again as Jesus shares so intimately from His Heart with me.

Weep, Evan, weep. Let your tears come for they are redemptive for My priest sons. Do not let your heart be hardened against your brother priests. Be always a bridge of mercy and understanding. I will ask of you much for your brother priests. Can you drink the cup that I give to you? A cup prepared by the Eternal Father and placed into My own Hands?

Jesus, you know all things. I give you my heart, yet my will and body are weak. But, yes Lord, I desire to drink of the cup and in so doing to be poured out as a holy libation. Yes Lord, I wish to drink of the cup. I receive now an image of Jesus the Good Shepherd with St. Pio on His left and St. Francis of Assisi on His right. Together they give me to drink of the cup. I sense four Guardian Angels surrounding me and now also, a fifth Guardian above me.

My son, drink then of the cup of mediation. Be poured out. Your role in the rebuilding of My Church will become clearer now. Your Eternal High Priest, Jesus

My Savior, be glorified in this poor vessel. I trust in You. I desire not to fear nor count the cost. I desire only one thing, to be placed in your Priestly Sacred Heart. Let me remain hidden here for all my days! I love you. Evan

July 20, 2004 – Into the Desert of Exile

My Jesus, I still wait upon Your kindness to enrich my parched soul with but a single word. I hunger to hear Your voice. My desire for Your love consumes me from within and how the enemy never ceases to assail me. Night and day he gives me over to torment. No rest. No comfort. There can be no relaxing of my watch as the enemy always spies upon me and from his unholy observation he plots my destruction! Jesus, save me! Open Your Heart to me and rescue me! Forget not Your love for Your priest son! My Mother, my confidence, please approach your Son on my behalf. Jesus, be welcomed into my heart. Yes, it is the most humble of abodes for Your Kingly nature, but have mercy on your servant.

Jesus speaks: **Come then, My son, abandon your fear and anxiety. Rejoice in My saving presence. Behold I make all things new. Live in this freedom, Evan. My beloved, great is My Love for you. Do not fear the enemy's machinations against you. I tell you his plotting never ceases against you, but in this** know your favor, your predilection. For from a young age you have given your fiat and now I draw you ever more deeply into the hidden recesses of My most tender, Sacred Heart.

My son, to what should I describe this present generation? Cannot they see the darkness that envelops their small and petty lives? Cannot they see the destruction that hems them in? Cannot they fathom the depth of My infinite mercy I extend to them? No, they are blind and fickle of heart. They cannot surrender their love to Me for they love their selves and their comforts, riches and evils, greater than I. I tell you they choose their own destruction, but the Heart of the Redeemer weeps all the same. They are Mine, entrusted to Me by the All Holy Eternal Father. Yet, these goats will not be led by My gentle voice. They reject My voice, My truth, My love. It is a most wicked age that thirsts for the blood of the most innocent. See the stain of this holocaust (abortion) upon the hands of nations. How long will I stay My Father's anger? Like Abraham, I beseech the Father to stay His Hand for but ten righteous men. And I search in vain!

My priest son, surrender to the voice of My Spirit. I call you now ever deeper into the desert of exile. Here your trust, your attentive will, and your sacrificial-agape love will be purified of the profanity of this wicked age. Leave your possessions behind and come to be possessed by the Healer of souls. Let us journey together deep into the Father's will. I will teach you of your Father and My Father. Let us venture forth obedient to the Spirit's call.

I forever love you, My son, with the love of a brother, a father, a dearest confidant-friend. Let us stay in one another's company. **Your Beloved Jesus**

I am Yours, my Beloved. How my heart races as I hear Your voice. Evan

September 11, 2004 – A Heart Well Suited

Yesterday I was in a clergy meeting and I was moved to pray in intercession for this company of priests and for our bishop. I prayed from the depths of mourning for the mortal wounds inflicted upon this priestly fraternity. Blessed Mother please be my Mediatrix of Grace. Channel the graces of the Trinity into the souls of our bishops and my brother priests. May your gentle, sweet voice correct and lead to a conversion from their ways of the world unto the Way of the Cross. Dear Lady, strengthen me your littlest priest! Let me not fall into despair but may I remain as a "stop-gap" in intercession for priests. With your help dear Mother, I can accomplish this great test of fidelity to the Father's will.

Jesus speaks: **My son Evan in whom I delight, I speak to you this morning from the depths of My Priestly Heart. You are experiencing very intimately now the sorrow of My Heart for the disorder of My presbyterate that is far from My Priestly Heart; far from My mind, thoughts, desires for the course of My Bride. I share with you My Heart that is wounded continually from My sons who have forgotten Me in their ministry done in My Name. Do you not feel the sting of this mockery, this empty betrayal of My Kingship, My prophetic Voice, My Priestly service? Evan, I have granted this position to you so that you might be drawn into a greater vision of the need of My brothers. I do this so that your heart may not grow cold, indifferent, or abandon itself to despair, but so that you might have the mind of a pure intercessor for this wound to My most delicate Sacred Heart.**

Again, will you be that balm? This is what I ask of you, to bring sweet consolation to Me by your own suffering as a victim lamb. Remain meek in the face of darkness and cruelty and you shall soar in your union to the Eternal Three. Love your

brother priests. **Allow My Mother to enlarge your heart, for how she does love her priest sons, consecrated, ordained into My own image. My son, implore the mediation of she who is the Mediatrix of all Grace.**

You wonder why I would call you to this apostolate for priests, yes?

Yes Lord, you know my inherent weakness in this regard.

It is because you have a heart that has been broken open by the wounds of the ones I call you to love. How great is your intercession, then, for those you find difficult to love on the natural level. I am asking you to come higher. Be seated with Our Lady and plan together the course of mediation for our priest sons. Always invoke her under her title, *Mary, Mother of Priests, Our Advocate and Mediatrix,* **please pray for your priest sons. She will open wide the channels of grace to drench those parched and aching souls of priests. Her mediation will usher in a new springtime in the Church! Believe in this My son. Do not continue in your disbelief, but believe. I bless you this day My little priest son. Be on Our Lady's errands now. Your Divine Master and friend, Jesus**

October 5, 2004 – Here is Your Protection

Lord Jesus, my prayer meditation has brought me here at the foot of Your cross as the soldiers pounded each nail into Your limbs; the merciless concussion pierces my being. For love of me alone You are pierced open with blunt nails. Your sinew and your muscle torn, You are opened up for love of me. But look now how sweetly You come to me. My heart is bathed, pierced by rays of Your love. My heart is opened with the key of love that You alone possess. I am bound by Your infinite love. Your love bolted you to a tree. You suffered long agonizing hours trying to get a breath. I am laid low, sorrowful to know how imperfect is my love for you as I stand at Your cross of Love. Lord Jesus, let me not leave this place. Bring me here each day. When I am tempted, when I am tepid, when I am indifferent, bring me to this place. Let my tears be mingled with Your blood. Mary stands with me. You have entrusted her to me. Lord Jesus, may my heart be opened, my arms outstretched and pierced, my gaze fixed upon your crucified love.

The Holy Spirit now shows me that I fear the loss of my good name, reputation. I fear being a fool for Christ. I see now the placard above Jesus on the cross. In my share of the Passion will my true name alone be known.

Jesus speaks: **My Spirit gathers you to stand at My cross with Mary, Our Mother. She will teach you sublimely at the school of My cross. She positions your hands in loving adoration. She fixes your gaze upon My sacred wounds. She bares your heart to receive Mine. She teaches you to hear and understand my sermon of love preached from the cross. Now all is readied. Show me your palms and your feet. Let them be pierced. Let yourself be fixed to My cross. Here is your protection. Here alone is your glory before men.**

October 7, 2004 – Our Lady of the Rosary

I hear the Eternal Father during my praying the Rosary with a beloved friend: **Evan, take up the pen and write. It is I your Eternal Father who speaks with you as you pray with my chosen little daughter. My son, it pleases the Heavenly Court greatly to see your fidelity to this appointed hour of grace for your combined souls. Know that with great delight I bestow many graces to your souls in this hour. I, who am your Father, who delights in your coming to Me as little ones, my children who are most attentive to My bidding and desirous of My Paternal** embrace.

Dear children, with fond memory the Universal Church recalls the role of the Chosen Daughter of Israel in the course of nations and the guidance of the Bark of Peter, *Mater Ecclesia*. She who is Immaculately Conceived has been chosen as the vessel of Immaculate graces channeled through her Motherly embrace of all Earth's children. How it delights the Eternal Father to see the fecundity of Our graces pass through the Immaculate One to nurture and foster the eternal life that has been given to your souls. She, who is the Immaculate One, in her eternal fiat brought forth the eternal fecundity of the Hypostatic Union of God and Man. She by her fiat continues to bring forth eternal fecundity in the soul of the believer, who has recourse to her Immaculate Heart.

On this day in which the Universal Church honors the glorious mediation of she who is the *Lady of the Rosary*, believe in the consecration of this simple prayer of the Rosary that echoes with the profound mysteries of salvation. The Hand of the Eternal Father has blessed this simplest of prayers for His children. It is the prayer of a child so that you might come to Me as a child. How I delight in My children who kneel in honor of her, the Mediatrix of All Grace, and who are most desirous to trust in My Paternal care.

Know that I bless you My children for your hearts have chosen the better part. I raise up the lowly to confound the proud. See My grace that flows freely into your souls. Rejoice in the Father's goodness, yes? Our Lady, Queen of Heaven and Earth, Our Lady of the Rosary blesses her little ones along with the Prince of Peace. Pray for peace. Pray for the protection of the sanctity of the Father's Life for all His children. I do love My Creation. Be of My fecundity, bring forth life and bring Me joy and glory. Your Eternal Father

Thank you, Father! Is this truly You? The tone is so sweet and paternal. I understand more clearly now that only as a child can we come to know, as through a veil, Your true nature, as Father! We love our Eternal Father. Evan

Chapter Three

Canticles of Heaven

I received these sung canticles from my Guardian Angel on Feasts and Solemnities of the Church. What joy is ours to join with all the Choirs of Angels and the Company of Saints to raise our voices in sung praise of the Thrice Holy One during our celebration of the Wedding Feast of the Lamb. Can we imagine the unfathomable beauty of the Heavenly Liturgy to which we are all one day invited!

$$\overline{IC} \quad \overline{XC}$$
$$NI \quad KA$$

November 21, 2003 - Feast of the Presentation of Mary – **Simeon's Canticle to the Mary Child**

Through my Guardian Angel on this tender Feast of Our Lady, I hear the holy prophet Simeon sing this canticle with great love and devotion.

See now the Ancient of Days has come to His People
Through His chosen daughter of Israel;
See now she comes to His Temple!
Adorned in garments of immortality.
She is His chosen Instrument;
She is the all holy pure one—
No fault, no blemish, no imperfection.

From the Heart of the Eternal High Priest

Hers is a perfect solicitude,
Hers is a perfect comeliness,
Hers is a perfect stature of grace.
All generations shall call her blessed!

The Most High God now stoops from the Heavens;
He has overshadowed His little one in her perfect humility and
docility.
From all eternity He has rejoiced in her splendor.
Such a continence of Beauty!
Even the Creator weeps for joy!
But see now her destiny is hidden,
For from within her hidden glory shall come forth the
Hope of all ages.
Discern now by God's Spirit—
She is God's Beauty and from her beauty comes the
King of all ages.

Welcome her then you Holy Temple!
For by her womb all shall become a living temple of the
Most High God.
God's Goodness is for all ages;
His Mercy is without end.
The People of Israel cry out your name this day!
Welcome, Miriam!

December 8, 2003 - Feast of the Immaculate Conception – **Canticle of The Immaculate One**

I receive this canticle of joy from my Guardian Angel on this great Feast of Our Lady.

Rejoice you Heavens and you who dwell therein!
Rejoice you who dwell upon the Earth!
Rejoice all of Creation!
Rejoice you stars above the seas!
Rejoice you mountains and you clouds!
Rejoice you valleys and you streams!
Rejoice you beasts, wild and tamed!
Rejoice all of creation!

For she the Immaculate One,
From all ages the chosen instrument of salvation,
Is now arrayed in beauty and glory.
See now the myriad of Angelic attendants
Prepare the Bride, the Chosen Daughter, the Mother,
Before all of the Heavenly Court!
She is received in loving worship (hyperdulia[1])
Before the very throne of the Thrice Holy Eternal Godhead!

All of the white robed Saints and the holy Martyrs in festive at-
tire,
As one holy body they press upon her throne;
They in one holy voice acclaim:
'Salve! Salve! Salve Regina!
Immaculate! Immaculate and Holy One!
All generations call you blessed!
O Chosen Daughter of Israel,
You are the one full of grace!
Miriam! Miriam! Miriam!

Extend your hands and release the rays of your Son's grace
Upon your earthly children!
Gather them into the folds of Your mantle
By the fragrance of your holiness and your purity
Draw them to yourself

---

[1] Hyperdulia is defined as veneration or worship given to the Virgin Mary as the most exalted of mere creatures. It is a higher veneration than dulia, which is given to the Saints. Only latria worship is given to the Trinity.

From the Heart of the Eternal High Priest

All Glory be to the Father
To the Son
To the Holy Spirit
Forever, Amen!

I also received a series of interior images. I saw Our Lady adorned in her festive robe and presented to the Heavenly Court. The saints and martyrs moved as one body towards her. All of Heaven sings to Our Lady. Our Lady is presented to the Trinity. After some time, I myself am presented to Our Lady. I see her face! Such beauty! Her entire being radiates the Light of the Trinity. Her hair is dark brown, her eyes the blue of the deep sea. Her skin is translucent ivory. Her nose is narrow and regal. Her lips are small. She is petite, so small. She is a young woman. She extends her hands to me! Then from her noble hands I see rays of grace coming upon me and then upon the Earth.

Dear Mother, keep me always as your little son of Nazareth. I consecrate myself to your service once again this day. *Ave Maria*!

December 24, 2003 - Christmas Eve - **Canticle of the Nativity**

I received this Canticle from my Guardian Angel on Christmas Eve. Such rejoicing in Heaven!

Praise to You Lord Jesus Christ!

Come let us gather, ye Heavenly Hosts;
Let us proclaim our glad tidings this night.
He who is the Lord of all Ages,
He who is the Ancient of Days,
He has shattered the veil of our darkness;
He will open to us Heaven's Gate!

Israel, she has kept watch with an ancient expectancy,
And now all nations, all creation
Share in the fullness of her joy
How sweet the embrace of our Savior to our human flesh!
For He, the Incarnate Word, is now one with our flesh.
In absolute stillness of night You were born.
Amidst thunder, earthquake and trumpet blast You shall return.

O mystery! O mystery!
The Creator now one with His creatures!
See now in the hillside from the cave,
His Light pierces the darkness of night.
His Light the sign to Ahaz, the promise of Isaiah:
The Virgin shall conceive and bear a child
And shall name Him Emmanuel—
The Hope of all generations.

Be then drawn by His Holy Light.
Be drawn by His most fair Virgin Mother.
Be drawn by His most gentle Guardian, Joseph.
Be drawn by the poverty of His birth in a stable.
Be drawn by the Angels' joyous song that fills the night sky.
Be drawn near this night from your far off places.
Let the Child's Mercy and Love shatter your darkness.
Let your hardened hearts be rent;
Let your heart sing!
For joy is your possession—
Joy is your gift to others.

The miracle is true this night—
See now the gentle Babe of Bethlehem in the manger;
He holds out His little arms to you;
He looks into your eyes and looks as if to cry,
For He stooped from the heavens to become a vulnerable child.
Will you not stoop down to pick Him up and embrace Him
To hold Him close to your heart?
Feel His warmth and fragile weight;

From the Heart of the Eternal High Priest

He rests in your embrace.
Will your heart not welcome Him as a soft pure manger?
Will you not give the Child comfort this night?
Will you not give Him an abode to rest in your very soul?

Let now His peace fill you this night;
It is His goodly desire.
Our Good King has arrived;
Let us make haste to welcome Him!
Bethlehem, Bethlehem, shine your light into my heart this night,
For His Holy Name this night is Mercy
Receive now as the reward of His obedience
His grace into your heart.
As He surrendered all things to the Father
For the sake of your love,
So now you surrender all things to the Savior
For the sake of His Love.

Oh wonderful exchange!
Miracle of heaven and earth this night!
As I receive the gift of the Christ Child this night,
Please now, I pray, receive me as my gift to you this night.
My heart is ready O God,
My heart is ready.
Come, ye Heavens, open your portals!
Sing with us, ye Angels, our salvation song:
Glory to God in the Highest and
Peace to His people on earth!

Jesus, my Good King,
Truly my heart rejoices in the gift of Your Incarnation.
I surrender to the mystery of Your Love.
May Love's embrace pierce my heart
With wonder, hope, and renewed strength.
Let all things be reconciled in my heart,
All past sins forgiven,
All past harms forgotten.
Make of me a new creation!

Let me be born anew
In this most gentle stable of Bethlehem,
Amidst the warmth, love, and light of the Holy Family.

Praise be to you, Lord Jesus Christ!